Anti-Achitophel

(1682)

THREE VERSE REPLIES TO

Absalom and Achitophel by JOHN DRYDEN

Absalom Senior by **Elkanah Settle**

Poetical Reflections by **Anonymous**

Azaria and Hushai by **Samuel Pordage**

FACSIMILE REPRODUCTIONS
EDITED WITH AN INTRODUCTION
BY

HAROLD WHITMORE JONES

GAINESVILLE, FLORIDA

SCHOLARS' FACSIMILES & REPRINTS

1961

SCHOLARS' FACSIMILES & REPRINTS
118 N.W. 26TH STREET
GAINESVILLE, FLORIDA
HARRY R. WARFEL, GENERAL EDITOR

REPRODUCED FROM COPIES IN

BRITISH MUSEUM

UNIVERSITY OF FLORIDA LIBRARY

L.C. CATALOG CARD NUMBER: 60-6430

MANUFACTURED IN THE U.S.A.
LETTERPRESS BY J. N. ANZEL, INC.
PHOTOLITHOGRAPHY BY EDWARDS BROTHERS
BINDING BY UNIVERSAL-DIXIE BINDERY

INTRODUCTION

English verse allegory, humorous or serious, political or moral, has deep roots; a reprint such as the present is clearly no place for a discussion of the subject at large:[1] it need only be recalled here that to the age that produced *The Pilgrim's Progress* the art form was not new. Throughout his life Dryden had his enemies, Prior and Montague in their satire of *The Hind and the Panther,* for example. The general circumstances under which Dryden wrote *Absalom and Achitophel,* familiar enough and easily accessible, are therefore recalled only briefly below. Information is likewise readily available on his use of Biblical allegory.[2]

We are here concerned with three representative replies to *Absalom and Achitophel:* their form, their authors, and details of their publication. Settle's poem was reprinted with one slight alteration a year after its first appearance; the *Reflections* has since been reprinted in part, Pordage's poem not at all. *Absalom Senior* has been chosen because, of the many verse pieces directed against Dryden's poem, it is of the greatest intrinsic merit and shows the reverse side of the medal, as it were, to that piece; the second is given, not for any literary merit it may possess — indeed, from its first appearance it has been dismissed as of small worth — but rather as a poem representative of much of the versifying that followed hard on the Popish Plot and as one that has inspired great speculation as to its author; the third, in addition to throwing light on the others, is a typical specimen of the lesser work produced in the Absalom dispute.

The author and precise publication date of the *Reflections* remain unidentified. Ascription of the poem to Buckingham rests ultimately on the authority of Wood's *Athenae Oxonienses* and on Wood alone, and we do not know on what evidence he thought it to be Buckingham's; we do know, however, that Wood was often mistaken over such matters. Sir Walter Scott in his collected edition of Dryden (1808; IX, 272-5) also accepted Buckingham as the author, but cited no authority; he printed extracts, yet the shortcomings of his edition, whatever its convenience, are well known. The poem has not appeared in any subsequent edition of Dryden's poems, the latest being the

---

1. Cf. E. D. Leyburn, *Satiric Allegory, Mirror of Man* (New Haven, 1956).
2. e.g., *Absalom's Conspiracy,* a tract tracing how the Bible story came to be used for allegorical purposes. See *The Harleian Miscellany* (1811), VIII, 478-479; and R. F. Jones, "The Originality of 'Absalom and Achitophel,'" *Modern Language Notes,* XLVI (April, 1931) 211-218.

four volume set (Oxford, 1958); the volume of the California Dryden relevant to *Absalom* is still awaited. Internal evidence is even more scanty. Only one passage of the *Reflections* (sig. D2) may bear on the matter. Perhaps the "Three-fold Might" (p. 7, line 11) refers, not to the poet's "tripartite design" (p. 7, line 10) or to the Triple Alliance of England, Holland, and Sweden against France (1677/8, as in *Absalom and Achitophel*, line 175) but either to a treatise which had occasioned some stir in the scientific world some twenty years previously: "the Delphic problem" proposed by Hobbes to the Royal Society on the duplication of the cube, which might have come to the ears of Buckingham as well as to those of the court,[3] or perhaps to the triple confederacy of Essex, Halifax, and Sunderland.[4] But to the Restoration reader the phrase "Three-fold Might" would rather have suggested the Triple Alliance, to which Dryden reverts in *The Medal* (lines 65-68) when he claims that Shaftesbury, "thus fram'd for ill, . . . loos'd our Triple Hold" on Europe.[5]

Evidence against Buckingham's authorship, on the other hand, is comparatively strong. The piece does not appear in his collected *Works* (1704-5). It surely would have been included even though he had at first wished to claim any credit from its publication and later have wished to disown it. Little connection, furthermore, will be found between the *Reflections* and the rest of his published verse or with the plays, including *The Rehearsal*, if the latter be his alone, which is doubtful.

Poetical Reflections has been ascribed to Edward Howard. W. Thomas Lowndes in his *Bibliographer's Manual* (1864; II, 126) assigned to this minor writer, on the authority of an auction note, the little collection *Poems and Essays, with a Paraphrase on Cicero's Laelius, or, Of Friendship . . . By a Gentleman* (1674), and G. Thorn-Drury, on the equally debatable evidence of an anonymous manuscript ascription on the title page of his own copy, ascribed the *Poetical Reflections* to Howard.[6] An examination of the *Poems and Essays*, however, reveals no point of resemblance with our poem. How, then, does Howard fit into the picture? He was in the rival camp to Dryden and was a friend of Martin Clifford[7] and of Thomas Sprat, then Buckingham's chaplain: these three have been thought to be jointly responsible for *The Rehearsal*. Sprat had published a poem of congratulation to Howard on Howard's *The British Princes* (1669), the latter a long pseudo-

3. Hobbes, *English Works* (1845), ed. by Molesworth, VII, 59-68.

4. H. C. Foxcroft, *A Character of the Trimmer* (Cambridge, England, 1946), p. 70. This book is an abridged version of the same author's *Life and Works of Halifax* (1897).

5. Cf. the phrase "Twofold might" in *Absalom and Achitophel*, I, 175.

6. *Review of English Studies*, I (1925) 82-83.

7. In his *Notes upon Mr. Dryden's Poems in Four Letters* (1687) Clifford, in 16 pages, accuses Dryden of plagiarism, especially in *Almanzor*.

epic of the Blackmore style in dreary couplets which, again, provides no parallel with the *Reflections*. And what of Howard's plays? Many of these were written in the 1660's during his poetic apprenticeship; none seems akin to our poem. Whereas, as shown in the Table of Allusions below, two independent readers often agreed over the identities of many characters in Settle's poem, Restoration readers at large were reticent over the authorship of the *Reflections*. Hugh Macdonald, in his useful *John Dryden: a Bibliography* (1939), was wise to follow their example, and it seems rash, therefore, to propose any new candidate in the face of such negative evidence. The poem exists in two states, apparently differing only in the title page.

Evidence of Settle's authorship of *Absalom Senior*, on the other hand, is neither wanting nor disputed. We have had to wait until our own century for the pioneer work on this writer, since he cannot have been considered a sufficiently major poet by Samuel Johnson's sponsors, and Langbaine's account is sketchy. In a periodical paper[8] Macdonald summarized supplementary evidence on the dates of composition of Settle's poem; he was working on it in January 1681/2, and it was published on the following April 6. Lockyer, Dean of Peterborough, asserted to Joseph Spence, who includes the rumor in *Anecdotes,* that Settle was assisted by Clifford and Sprat and by "several best hands of those times";[9] but Spence is notoriously unreliable. In the lack of other evidence, then, it seems best to take the poem as wholly Settle's. It needs only to add a few words on its textual states. The First Edition, here reproduced, seems to exist in a single impression, and likewise the Second Edition of the Settle (1682, in quarto) seems to have been struck off in a single textual state. Of its individual variants from the First Edition only the following seem of any significance and, since there is no reason to suppose that it was printed from any copy other than the First, they may be merely the result of carelessness.

FIRST EDITION	SECOND EDITION
p. 3, line 4, enthron'd, with	inthron'd with
3 8, Arts . . . steps	Art's . . . step's
11 10, Rods;	Rods?
13 26, to Descend	do Descend
14 17, couch,	couch
29 9, Cedar	Cedars
31 21, Temples	Temple

8. "The Attacks on John Dryden," *Essays and Studies by Members of the English Association,* XXI, 41-74.

9. Joseph Spence, *Anecdotes . . . of Books and Men* (1858), p. 51.

For "No Link . . . night" (p. 35, lines 19-24), the Second Edition substitutes, for an undetermined reason, the following:

> No less the Lordly Zelecks Glory sound
> For courage and for Constancy renoun'd:
> Though once in naught but borrow'd plumes adorn'd,
> So much all servile Flattery he scorn'd;
> That though he held his Being and Support,
> By that weak Thread the Favour of a Court,
> In Sanhedrims unbrib'd, he firmly bold
> Durst Truth and Israels Right unmov'd uphold;
> In spight of Fortune, still to Honour wed,
> By Justice steer'd, though by Dependence fed.

Very little can be said of Pordage's poem, beyond its date of publication (January 17, 1681/2)[10] and the fact that no parallel has been found with his earlier work. As no detailed study on him, published or unpublished, has been traced, we can only have recourse to the standard works on the period; data thus easily accessible are not therefore reproduced here. A so-called second edition (MacDonald 205b) is identical with the first.

In conclusion a few comments may be made on the general situation into which the poems fit. It will be remembered that *Absalom and Achitophel* appeared after the Exclusion Bill, the purpose of which was to debar James Duke of York from the Protestant succession, had been rejected by the House of Lords, mainly through the efforts of Halifax. Dryden's poem was advertised on November 17, 1681, and we may safely assume that it was published only a short time before Settle and our other authors were hired by the Whigs to answer it. Full details have not survived; one suspects Shaftesbury's Green Ribbon Club. That such replies were considered necessary testifies both to the popularity of *Absalom and Achitophel* with the layman in politics and to the Whigs' fear of its harming their cause. Settle's was of course a mercenary pen, and it is amusing to note that after ridiculing Halifax here he was quite prepared to publish, fourteen years later, *Sacellum Apollinare: a Funeral Poem to the Memory of that Great Statesman, George Late Marquiss of Halifax,* and on this count his place among Pope's Dunces seems merited. In tracing his quarrel with Dryden up to the publication of *Absalom Senior,* critics have tended to overlook the fact that by 1680 there was already hostility between the two;[11] less has been said about the effect on Dryden of the poets themselves. The spleen of his contributions to the Second Part of *Absalom and Achitophel* is essentially a manufactured one and for the public entertainment; personally he was comparatively unmoved — the Og portrait,

10. *Modern Philology,* XXV (1928) 409-416.
11. e.g., over *The Empress of Morocco;* see Scott's *Dryden,* XV, 397-413.

for example, is less representative than his words in "The Epistle to the Whigs" prefixed to *The Medal.* Here, as in *Mac Flecknoe,* he appears to have been able to write vituperation to order. "I have only one favor to desire of you at parting," he says, and it is "that when you think of answering this poem, you would employ the same pens against it, who have combated with so much success against *Absalom and Achitophel;* for then you may assure yourselves of a clear victory, without the least reply." Is it for the best that this forecast proved the right one?

For permission to reproduce their copies of texts comprising the present reprint thanks are expressed to the University of Florida Library (*Absalom Senior*) and to the Trustees of the British Museum (the other two poems). The University of Leeds and the City of Manchester Public Library are also thanked for leave to use contemporary marginalia in each's copy of Settle's poem. The provenance of the latter two copies of this piece is unknown; the first, now in the Brotherton Collection, bears the name William Crisp on its last blank leaf and, in abbreviated form, identifies some characters; the second, of unidentified ownership, is fuller.

HAROLD WHITMORE JONES

Liverpool, England
November, 1959

TABLE OF ALLUSIONS

NAMES

The persons and places referred to in the allegories are identified in the following lists of names. M indicates the ascription in the Manchester copy; B, that in the Leeds University copy. Within the list for each poem, names similarly used in *Absalom and Achitophel* are omitted; those used with a different meaning are marked with an asterisk.

ABSALOM SENIOR

Absalom, Duke of York
Achitophel, Halifax
Adriel, Earl of Huntington
Amasai, Earl of Macclesfield (M, B)
Amnon, Godfrey
Amiel, Buckingham (B)
Amram, Sir William Jones
Arabia, Portugal

Ashur, Fourth Lord Herbert of Cherbury (M)
Babylon, Rome
Barak, Drake
Barzillai, Shaftesbury (B)
Caleb, Laurence Hyde, son of Clarendon (B)

Camries, Third Lord Howard of Escrick (M)
°Corah, Sir Edward Seymour (B)
Deborah, Queen Elizabeth
Endor, Oxford (B)
Geshur, Ireland
Hanaan, Lord Nottingham
Hazor, Spain
°Helon, First Duke of Bedford
°Hothriel, Slingsby Bethell
°Hushai, Earl of Argyll
Ithream, Monmouth
Jabin, Philip II

°Jonas, ?Sir William Gregory (M glosses as Seymour; see Corah)
°Jotham, Earl of Essex
Laura, Anne Reeve
Levitick chiefs, English bishops (B)
Micah, Sir William Williams, Speaker of the Commons
°Nadab, Lauderdale
°Shimei, Jeffreys (B)
Sidon, Denmark
Sisera, Medina Sidonia
Zeleck, unidentified

POETICAL REFLECTIONS

°Amiel, ?Finch, Lord Chancellor
°Bathsheba, ?Queen Catherine

Nimrod, Cromwell
Tory Roger, L'Estrange

AZARIA AND HUSHAI

Abidon, unidentified
Amalack, ?Henry Hyde, son of Clarendon
Amazia, Charles II
Aminadab, Ashur, unidentified; see Ashur above.
Athalia, Mary Queen of Scots
Azaria, Monmouth
Azyad, Sir Edmundbury Godfrey
Bibbai, L'Estrange
Canaanites, Chemarim, Papists
Doeg, Danby
Edomites, Irish
Elam, Lawrence Hyde, Earl of Rochester
Eliab, Lord Russell
Eliakim, Duke of York
Elishama, ?Macclesfield
Elizur, Enan, unidentified
Essens, nonconformists
Gamaliel, unidentified

Gedaliah, Edward Coleman
Gibbar, ?Lord Clifford
Harim, ?Lord Wharton
Helon, Bedford
°Hushai, Shaftesbury
Jehosaphat, Henry VII
Jeptha, see Settle, p. 21
Jerusha, Anne, Countess of Buccleuch
Joash, Charles I
Jocoliah, Lucy Walters
°Jotham, ?Halifax
Libni, Oates
Muppim, ?Lauderdale
Nashai, Essex
Pagiel, unidentified
Pharisee, high churchman
Rehoboam, unidentified
°Shimei, Dryden
Zabed, Cromwell
Zattue, unidentified

REFERENCES

Biblical parallels and parallels with *Absalom and Achitophel* are omitted. The *Dedications* of the poems can be compared with Dryden's in *Absalom and Achitophel*.

ABSALOM SENIOR

PAGE

3: *Barak.* The only borrowing in the poem from a popular seventeenth century jest book, *Wits Recreations* (1640), "Epigrams," no. 46, "On Sir Fr. Drake": "The sun itself cannot forget/His fellow traveller."

11: a *Jewish* Renegade. Cardinal Philip Thomas Howard (B).

13: a Breaden God. Either a reference to transubstantiation (see also II Kings 2-3 and II Chron. 34) or an allusion to the Meal Tub Plot (1679).

16: a Cake of *Shew-bread.* In addition to the Biblical allusion, perhaps a reference to the poisoning of the Holy Roman Emperor Henry VII by the communion wafer.

17: in Possession. As this legal term is opposed to "reversion" emendation is unnecessary.

19: to bear. There was a belief that Jeffreys was connected with the Duchess of Portsmouth (B). The "Golden Prize" was perhaps protestantism, to be suppressed under a secret provision of the Treaty of Dover (1670).

19: Court-Drugster. Sir George Wakeman.

25: beautifyed. *OED* notices this catachrestic form of "beatified"

32: All-be-devill'd Paper. Presumably that accusing Shaftsbury of high treason.

34: A Cell. Eton.

37: Midnight Bawd. Mrs. Cellier.

POETICAL REFLECTIONS

4: Ignoramus. the jury's verdict at Shaftesbury's trial.

5: the Joyner. Stephen Colledge.

9: motly Sight. read "Spight"?

AZARIA AND HUSHAI

10: Power on *Amazia.* Read "of *Amazia*"?

19: allay'd. Read "ally'd"?

28: to board. Read "hoard"?

38: swifty back. So in all copies seen.

Abſalom Senior:

OR,

ACHITOPHEL

TRANSPROS'D.

A

POEM.

Si Populus vult decipi, &c.

LONDON:

Printed for *S. E.* and Sold by *Langley Curtis* , at the Sign of
Sir *Edmondbury Godfrey,* near *Fleetbridge.* 1682.

To the TORIES.

Entlemen, *for so you all write your selves ;
and indeed you are your own Heralds ,
and Blazon all your Coats with* Honour
and Loyalty *for your* Supporters ; *nay,
and you are so unconscionable too in that
point, that you will allow neither of them
in any other* Scutcheons *but your own.*
But who has 'em , *or has* 'em *not , is not my present business ;
onely as you profess your selves* Gentlemen, *to conjure you to give
an Adversary fair play; and that if any person whatsoever shall
pretend to be aggrieved by this* POEM, *or any part of it, that
he would bear it patiently; since the Licentiousness of the first*
Absolom *and* Achitophel *has been the sole occasion of the Liberty of This, I having only taken the Measure of My Weapon ,
from the Length of his ; which by the Rules of Honour ought
not to offend you ; especially, since the boldness of that Ingenious
Piece, was wholly taken from the Encouragement you gave the
Author ; and 'tis from that Boldness only that this* POEM *takes
its Birth : for had not his daring Pen brought that Piece into
the World, I had been so far from troubling my self in any Subject on this kind, that I may justly say in one sence, the Writer of
that* Absolom, *is the Author of this. This favour, as in Justice due, obtain'd from you , I shall not trouble you with a long
Preface, like a tedious Compliment at the Door, but desire you to
look in for your Entertainment. Onely I cannot forbear telling
you, that one thing I am a little concern'd for you,* Tories, *that
your* Absoloms *and* Achitophels , *and the rest of your Grinning
Satyres against the* Whiggs, *have this one unpardonable Fault ,
That the Lash is more against a* David, *than an* Achitophel ;
whilst the running down of the PLOT *at so extravagant a rate,
favours of very little less (pardon the Expression) than ridiculing of Majesty it self, and turning all those several Royal Speeches
to the Parliament on that Subject, onely into those double-tongu'd
Oracles that sounded one thing, and meant another. Besides, after this unmannerly Boldness , of not onely branding the publick
Justice of the Nation, but affronting even the Throne it self, to*

push

The Epiſtle to the *TORIES*.

puſh the humour a little farther, you run into ten times a greater Vice, (and in the ſame ſtrain too) than what you ſo ſeverely inveigh againſt: and whilſt a *POPISH PLOT* through want of ſufficient Circumſtances, and credible Witneſſes, miſcarries with you, a *PROTESTANT PLOT* without either Witneſs or Circumſtance at all, goes currant. Nay you are ſo far now from your former niceties and ſcruples, and diſputing about raiſing of Armies, and not one Commiſſion found, that you can ſwallow the raiſing of a whole Proteſtant *ARMY*, without either Commiſſion, or Commiſſion-Officer; Nay, the very *When*, *Where*, and *How*, are no part of your Conſideration. Tis true, the great Cry amongſt you, is, The Nations Eyes are open'd; but I am afraid, in moſt of you, 'tis onely to look where you like beſt: and to help your lewd Eye-ſight, you have got a damnable trick of turning the *Perſpective* upon occaſion, and magnifying or diminiſhing at pleaſure. But alas, all talking to you is but impertinent, and ſending and proving ſignifie juſt nothing; for after all Arguments, both Parties are ſo irreconcileable, that as the Author of Abſolom wiſely obſerved, they'll be *Fools* or *Knaves* to each other to the end of the Chapter. And therefore I am ſo reaſonable in this point, that I ſhould be very glad to divide 'em between 'em, and give the Fool to the Tory, and the Knave to the Whigg. For the Tories that will believe no *POPISH PLOT*, may as juſtly come under that denomination, as They, that David tells us, ſaid in their Hearts there was no God. And then let the Whiggs that do believe a Popiſh Plot be the Knaves, for daring to endeavour to hinder the Effects of a Popiſh Plot, when the Tories are reſolved to the contrary. But to draw near a concluſion, I have one favour more to beg of you, that you'll give me the freedom of clapping but about a ſcore of years extraordinary on the back of my Abſolom. Neither is it altogether ſo unpardonable a Poetical Licenſe, ſince we find as great ſlips from the Author of your own Abſolom, where we ſee him bring in a Zimri into the Court of David, who in the Scripture-ſtory dyed by the Hand of Phineas in the days of Moſes. Nay, in the other extream, we find him in another place talking of the Martyrdome of Stephen, ſo many Ages after. And if ſo famous an Author can forget his own Rules of Unity, Time, and Place, I hope you'll give a Minor Poet ſome grains of Allowance, and he ſhall ever acknowledge himſelf

Your Humble Servant.

A B S O-

Abſalom Senior:

OR,

ACHITOPHEL

TRANSPROS'D.

IN Gloomy Times, when Prieſtcraft bore the ſway,
    And made Heav'ns Gate a Lock to their own Key :
    When ignorant Devotes did blindly bow ,
    And groaping to be ſav'd they knew not how :
Whilſt this *Egyptian* darkneſs did orewhelm,
The Prieſt ſate Pilot even at Empires Helm.
Then Royal Necks were yok'd, and Monarchs ſtill
Hold but their Crowns at his Almighty Will.
And to defend this high Prerogative,
Falſely from Heaven he did that powr derive :
By a Commiſſion forg'd i'th' hand of God,
Turn'd *Aarons* blooming wand, to *Moſes* ſnaky Rod.
Whilſt Princes little Scepters overpowr'd,
Made but that prey his wider Gorge devour'd.
Now to find Wealth might his vaſt pomp ſupply,
(For coſtly Roofs befit a Lord ſo high)
No Arts were ſpar'd his Luſter to ſupport,
But all Mines ſearcht t'enrich his ſhining Court.
Then Heav'n was bought, Religion but a Trade ;
And Temples Murder's Sanctuary made.
By *Phineas* Spear no bleeding *Cozbies* groan'd,
If *Cozbies* Gold for *Cozbies* Crimes aton'd.
With theſe wiſe Arts, (for Humane Policy
As well as Heav'nly Truth, mounts Prieſts ſo high)
'Twixt gentle Penance, lazy Penitence,
A Faith that gratifies both Soul and Senſe ;
With eaſie ſteps to everlaſting Bliſs,
He paves the rugged way to Paradice.

B   Thus

Thus almoſt all the Proſelyte-World he drives,
Whilſt th univerſal Drones buz to his Hives.
Implicite Faith Religion thus convey'd
Through little pipes to his great Channel laid,
Till Piety through ſuch dark Conduits led,
Was poyſon'd by the Spring on which it fed.
Here blind Obedience to a blinder Guide,
Nurſt that Blind Zeal that rais'd the Prieſtly pride ;
Whilſt to make Kings the Sovereign Prelate own,
Their Reaſon he enſlav'd, and then their Throne.
The Mitre thus above the Diadem ſoar'd,
Gods humble ſervant He, but Mans proud Lord.
It was in ſuch Church-light blind-zeal was bred,
By Faiths infatuating Meteor led ;
Blind Zeal, that can even Contradictions joyn ;
A Saint in Faith, in Life a Libertine ;
Makes Greatneſs though in Luxury worn down,
Bigotted even to th' Hazard of a Crown ;
Ty'd to the Girdle of a Prieſt ſo faſt,
And yet Religious only to the waſt.
But Conſtancy atoning Conſtancy,
Where that once raigns, Devotion may lye by.
T'eſpouſe the Churches Cauſe lyes in Heav'ns road,
More than obeying of the Churches God.
And he dares fight, for Faith is more renown'd
A Zealot Militant, than Martyr crown'd,
Here the Arch-Prieſt to that Ambition blown,
Pull'd down Gods Altars, to erect his own :
For not content to publiſh Heav'ns command,
The Sacred Law penn'd by th'Almighty Hand ,
And *Moſes*-like 'twixt God and *Iſrael* go,
Thought *Sinai's* Mount a Pinacle too low.
So charming ſweet were Incenſe fragrant Fumes,
So pleas'd his Noſtrils, till th'Aſpirer comes
From offering, to receiving Hecatombs ;
And ceaſing to adore, to be ador'd.
So fell Faiths guide : ſo loftily he towr'd,
Till like th'Ambitious *Lucifer* accurſt,
Swell'd to a God, into a Fiend he burſt.

But as great *Lucifer* by falling gain'd
Dominion , and ever in Damnation reign'd ;

And

And though from Lights bleft Orb for ever driven, ⎫
Yet Prince o'th'Air, h'had that vaft Scepter giv'n, ⎬
T'have Subjects far more numerous than Heav'n. ⎭
And thus enthron'd, with an infernal fpight,
The genuine Malice of the Realms of night,
The Paradife he loft blafphemes, abhors,
And againft Heav'n proclaims Eternal Wars ;
No Arts untry'd, no hoftile fteps untrod,
Both againft Truths Adorers, and Truths God.

So Faiths faln Guide, now *Baals* great Champion raign'd ;
Wide was his Sway, and Mighty his Command :
Whilft with implacable revenge he burn'd,
And all his Rage againft Gods *Ifrael* turn'd.
Here his invenom'd Souls black gall he flings,
Spots all his Snakes, and points his Scorpions ftings :
Omits no Force, or Treacherous Defigne,
Bleft *Ifrael* to affault, or undermine.
But the firft Sword did his keen Malice draw,
Was aim'd againft the God-like *Deborah.*
Deborah, the matchlefs pride of *Judah*'s Crown,
Whofe Female hand *Baal's* impious Groves cut down,
His banifht Wizards from her *Ifrael* thruft,
And pounded all their Idols into duft.
Her Life with indefatigable pain,
By Daggers long, and poyfons fought in vain :
At length they angry *Jabins* Rage enflam'd,
Hazors proud King, for Iron Chariots fam'd ;
A Warriour powerful, whofe moft dreadful Hoaft
Proclaim'd Invincible, (were humane Boaft
Infallible) by haughty *Sifera* led,
'Gainft *Deborah* their bloody Banners fpread.
Here *Deborah* her *Barak* calls to War ;
Barak, the Suns fam'd fellow-traveller,
Who wandring o're the Earths furrounded Frame,
Had travell'd far as his great Miftrefs Fame.
Here *Barak* did with *Deborah's* vengeance fly,
And to that fwift prodigious Victory,
So much by Humane Praifes undefin'd,
That Fame wants Breath, and Wonder lags behind.
To Heav'ns high Arch her founding Glories rung,
Whilft thus great ***Deborah*** and ***Barak*** fung.

Hear

HEar, *oh ye Princes, oh ye Kings give Ear,*
   And Israels *great Avengers honour hear.*
When God of Hosts, thou Israels *Spear and Shield,*
Wentst out of Seir, *and marched'st from* Edoms *field,*
Earth trembled, the Heaven's drop'd, the Clouds all pour'd ;
The Mountains melted from before the Lord ;
Even thy own Sinai *melted into streams,*
At Israels *dazling Gods refulgent Beams.*
In Shamgar *and in* Jael's *former days,*
The wandring Traveller walk'd through by-ways.
They chose new Gods. No Spear nor Sword was found,
To have Idolatry depos'd, Truth Crown'd,
Till I alone, against Jehovahs *Foes ;*
I Deborah, *I* Israels *Mother rose.*
Wake Deborah, *wake, raise thy exalted Head ;*
Rise Barak, *and Captivity Captive lead.*
For to blest Deborah, *belov'd of* Heav'n,
Over the Mighty is Dominion given.
Great Barak *leads, and* Israels *Courage warms ;*
Ephraim *and* Benjamin *march down in Arms :*
Zebulon *and* Nepthali *my Thunder bore,*
Dan *from her Ship, and* Asher *on the Shore.*
Behold Megiddoes *waves, and from afar,*
See the fierce Jabins *threatning storm of War.*
But Heav'n *'gainst* Sisera *fought, and the kind Stars*
Kindl'd their embattel'd Fires for Deborah's *Wars,*
Shot down their Vengeance that miraculous day,
When Kishons *Torrents swept their Hosts away.*
But curse ye Meroz, *curse 'em from on high,*
Did the denouncing voice of Angels cry ;
Accurst be they that went not out t'oppose
The Mighty Deborah's, God's, *and* Israel's *Foes.*
Victorious Judah! *Oh my Soul, th'hast trod,*
Trod down their strengths. So fall the Foes of God.
But they who in his Sacred Laws delight,
Be as the Sun when he sets out in might.

Thus sung, they conquer'd *Deborah* ; thus fell
Hers, and Heav'ns Foes. But no Defeat tames Hell.
By Conquest overthrown, but not dismay'd,
'Gainst *Israel* still their private Engines play'd.

                      And

And their dire Ma chinations to fulfil,
Their stings torn out, they kept their poyson still.
And now too weak in open force to joyn,
In close Cabals they hatcht a damn'd Design,
To light that Mine as should the world amaze,
And set the ruin'd *Israel* in a blaze.

When *Judahs* Monarch with his Princes round,
Amidst his glorious Sanedrim sate Crown'd ,
Beneath his Throne a Cavern low, and dark
As their black Souls, for the great Work they mark.
In this lone Cell their Midnight-Hands bestow'd
A *Stygian* Compound, a combustive load
Of Mixture wondrous, Execution dire,
Ready the Touch of their Infernal Fire.
Have you not seen in yon æthereal Road,
How at the Rage of th'angry driving God,
Beneath the pressure of his furious wheels
The Heav'ns all rattle, and the Globe all reels?
So does this Thunder's Ape its lightning play,
Keen as Heav'ns Fires, and scarce less swift than they.
A short-liv'd glaring Murderer it flies,
In Times least pulse, a Moments wing'd surprize ;
'Tis born, looks big, talks lowd, breaths death, and dies.
This Mixture was th'Invention of a Priest ;
The Sulphurous Ingredients all the best
Of Hells own growth : for to dire Compounds still
Hell finds the Minerals, and the Priest the Skill.

From this curst Mine they had that blow decreed,
A Moments dismal blast, as should exceed
All the Storms, Battles, Murders, Massacres,
And all the strokes of Daggers, Swords, or Spears,
Since first *Cain's* hand at *Abels* Head was lift :
A Blow more swift than Pestilence, more swift
Than ever a destroying Angel rod,
To pour the Vial of an angry God.

The Train was laid, the very Signal giv'n;
But here th'all-seeing, *Israels* Guardian, Heav'n
Could hold no longer ; and to stop their way,
With a kind Beam from th'Empyræan Day,

C

Disclosed

Difclos'd their hammering Thunder at the Forge;
And made their Cyclops Cave their Bolts difgorge.

Difcover'd thus, thus loft, betray'd, undone,
Yet ftill untir'd, the Reftlefs Caufe goes on;
And to retrieve a yet aufpicious day,
A glowing fpark even in their Afhes lay,
Which thus burft out in flames. In *Gefhur* Land,
The utmoft Bound of *Ifraels* Command,
Where *Judah's* planted Faith but flowly grew,
A Brutal Race that *Ifraels* God n'er knew:
A Nation by the Conquerors Mercy grac'd,
Their Gods preferv'd, and Temples undefac'd;
Yet not content with all the Sweets of Peace,
Free their Eftates, and free their Confciences;
'Gainft *Ifrael* thofe confederate Swords they drew,
Which with that vaft Affaffination flew
Two hundred thoufand Butcher'd Victims fhar'd
One common doom : No Sex nor Age was fpar'd :
Not kneeling Beauties Tears, not Virgins Cries,
Nor Infants Smiles : No prey fo fmall but dies.
Alas, the hard-mouth'd Blood-hound, Zeal, bites through;
Religion hunts, and hungry Jaws purfue.
To what ftrange Rage is Superftition driven,
That Man can outdo Hell to fight for Heav'n!
So Rebel *Gefhur* fought : fo drown'd in gore,
Even Mother Earth blufht at the Sons fhe bore;
And ftill afham'd of her old ftaining Brand,
Her Head fhrinks down and Quagmires half their Land.
Yet not this blow *Baals* Empire could enlarge
For *Ifrael* ftill was Heav'ns peculiar charge:
Unfhaken ftill in all this Scene of Blood,
Truths Temple firm on Golden Columns ftood.
Whilft *Sauls* Revenging Arm proud *Gefhur* fcourg'd,
From their rank foyl their *Hydra's* poyfon purg'd.

Yet does not here their vanquifh'd fpleen give o're,
But as untir'd, and reftlefs as before,
Still through whole waiting Ages they outdo
At once the Chimifts pains and patience too.
Who though he fees his burfting Limbecks crack,
And at one blaft, one fatal Minutes wrack,

The

The forward Hopes of sweating years expire ;
With sad, yet painful hand new lights his Fire :
Pale, lean, and wan, does Health, Wealth, all consume ;
Yet for the great Elixir still to come,
Toyls and hopes on. No less their Plottings cease ;
So hope, so toyl, the foes of *Israels* peace.

When lo, a long expected day appears,
Sought for above a hundred rowling years ;
A day i'th' register of Doom set down,
Presents 'em with an Heir of *Israels* Crown.
Here their vast hopes of the rich *Israels* spoils,
Requites the pains of their long Ages Toyls.
Baals Banners now i'th' face of day shall march,
With Heav'ns bright Roof for his Triumphal Arch.
His lurking Missioners shall now no more
From Forreign Schools in borrow'd shapes come o're ;
Convert by Moon-light, and their Mystick Rites
Preach to poor Female half-Soul'd Proselytes.
An all-commanding Dragon now shall soar,
Where the poor Serpents onely crawl'd before.
Baals Restoration, that most blest Design,
Now the great work of Majesty, shall shine,
Made by his consecrating hand Divine.
He shall new plant their Groves with each blest Tree,
A graft of an Imperial Nursery.
In the kind Air of this new *Eden* blest,
Percht on each bough, and Palaces their nest ;
No more by frighting Laws forc'd t'obscure flight,
And gloomy walks, like obscene Birds of Night ;
Their warbling Notes like *Philomel* shall sing,
And like the Bird of *Paradise* their wing.
Thus *Israels* Heir their ravisht Souls all fired ;
For all things to their ardent hopes conspired.

His very youth a Bigot Mother bred,
And tainted even the Milk on which he fed.
Him onely of her Sons design'd for *Baals*
Great Champion 'gainst *Jerusalems* proud Walls ;
Him dipt in *Stygian* Lake, by timely craft,
Invulnerable made against **Truths** pointed shaft.

But

But to confirm his early poyson'd Faith,
'Twas in the curſed Forreign Tents of *Gath*,
'Twas there that he was loſt. There *Abſolon*
By *Davids* fatal Baniſhment undone,
Saw their falſe Gods till in their Fires he burn'd,
Truths Manna, for *Egyptian* Fleſhpots, ſcorn'd.
Not *David* ſo ; for he Faiths Champion Lord,
Their Altars loath'd, and prophane Rites abhorr'd :
Whilſt his firm Soul on wings of *Cherubs* rod,
And tun'd his Lyre to nought but *Abrahams* God.
Thus the gay *Iſrael* her long Tears quite dry'd,
Her reſtor'd *David* met in all her Pride ,
Three Brothers ſaw by Miracle brought back,
Like *Noahs* Sons ſav'd from the worlds great wrack ;
An unbelieving *Ham* graced on each hand,
'Twixt God-like *Shem*, and pious *Japhet* ſtand.

'Tis true, when *David*, all his ſtorms blown o're,
Waſted by Prodigies to *Jordans* ſhore,
(So ſwift a Revolution, yet ſo calm)
Had cur'd an Ages wounds with one days Balm ;
Here the returning *Abſolon* his vows
With *Iſrael* joyns, and at their Altars bows.
Perhaps ſurpriz'd at ſuch ſtrange bleſſings ſhowr'd,
Such wonders ſhewn both t'*Iſraels* Faith, and Lord,
His Reſtoration-Miracle he thought
Could by no leſs than *Iſraels* God be wrought.
Whilſt the enlightned *Abſolon* thus kneels,
Thus dancing to the ſound of *Aarons* Bells,
What dazling Rays did *Iſraels* Heir adorn,
So bright his Sun in his unclouded Morn !
'Twas then his leading hand in Battle drew
'That Sword that *Davids* fam'd ten thouſand ſlew :
Davids the Cauſe, but *Abſolons* the Arm.
Then he could win all Hearts, all Tongues could charm :
Whilſt with his praiſe the ecchoing plains all rung,
A thouſand Timbrels play'd, a thouſand Virgins ſung ;
And in the zeal of every jocund Soul,
Abſolons Health with *Davids* crown'd one Bowl.

Had he fixt here, yes, Fate, had he fixt here,
To Man ſo Sacred, and to Heav'n ſo dear,

What

What could he want that Hands, Hearts, Lives could pay,
Or Tributary Worlds beneath his feet could lay ?
What Knees, what Necks to mount him to his Throne ;
What Gems, what Stars to sparkle in his Crown ?
So pleas'd, so charm'd, had *Israels* Genius smil'd ;
But oh the Pow'rs, by treacherous snakes beguil'd,
Into a more than *Adams* Curse he run,
Tasting that Fruit has *Israels* World undone.
Nay, wretched even below his falling state,
Wants *Adams* Eyes to see his *Adams* Fate.
In vain was *Davids* Harp and *Israels* Quire ;
For his Conversion all in vain conspire :
For though their influence a while retires,
His own false Planets were th'Ascendant Fires.
Heav'n had no lasting Miracle design'd ;
It did a while his fatal Torrent bind.
As *Joshua's* Wand did *Jordan's* streams divide,
And rang'd the watry Mountains on each side.
But when the marching *Israel* once got o're,
Down crack the Chrystal Walls the Billows pow'r,
And in their old impetuous Channel roar.

   At this last stroke thus totally o'rethrown,
Apostasie now seal'd him all her own.
Here ope'd that gaping Breach, that fatal door,
Which now let in a thousand Ruines more.
All the bright Virtues, and each dazling Grace,
Which his rich Veins drew from a God-like Race ;
The Mercy, and the Clemency Divine,
Those Sacred Beams which in mild *David* shine ;
Those Royal Sparks, his Native Seeds of Light,
Were all put out, and left a Starless Night.
A long farewel to all that's Great and Brave :
Not Cataracts more headstrong ; as the Grave
Inexorable ; Sullen and Untun'd
As Pride depos'd ; scarce *Lucifer* dethron'd
More Unforgiving ; his enchanted Soul
Had drank so deep of the bewitching Bowl,
Till he whose hand, with *Judahs* Standart, bore
Her Martial Thunder to the *Tyrian* shore,
Arm'd in her Wars, and in her Laurels crown'd ;
Now all forgotten at one stagg'ring wound,

D

Falling

Falling from *Israels* Faith ; from *Israels* Caufe,
Peace, Honour, Int'reft, all at once withdraws:
Nor is he deaf t'a Kingdoms Groans alone,
But could behold ev'n *Davids* fhaking Throne ;
David, whofe Bounty rais'd his glittering Pride,
The Bafis of his Glories Pyramide.
But Duty, Gratitude, all ruin'd fall :
Zeal blazes, and Oblivion fwallows all.
So *Sodom* did both burnt and drown'd expire ;
A poyfon'd Lake fucceeds a Pile of Fire.

On this Foundation *Baals* laft Hope was built,
The fure Retreat for all their Sallying Guilt :
A Royal Harbour, where the rowling Pride
Of *Israels* Foes might fafe at Anchor ride ;
Defie all Dangers, and even Tempefts fcorn,
Though *Judahs* God fhould Thunder in the Storm.

Here *Israels* Laws, the dull Levitick Rolls,
At once a clog to Empire, and to Souls,
Are the firft Martyrs to the Fire they doom,
To make great *Baals* Triumphant Legends room.
But ere their hands this glorious work can Crown,
Their long-known Foe the Sanedrin muft down ;
Sanedrins the Free-born *Israels* Sacred Right,
That God-like Ballance of Imperial Might ;
Where Subjects are from Tyrant-Lords fet free,
From that wild Thing unbounded man would be ;
Where Pow'r and Clemency are poys'd fo even,
A Conftitution that refembles Heav'n.
So in th'united great T H R E E - O N E we find
A Saving with a Dooming Godhead joyn'd.
(But why, oh why! if fuch reftraining pow'r
Can bind Omnipotence, fhould Kings wifh more?)
A Conftitution fo Divinely mixt,
Not Natures bounded Elements more fixt.
Thus Earths vaft Frame with firm and folid ground,
Stands in a foaming Ocean circled round ;
Yet This not overflowing, That not drown'd.
But to rebuild their Altars, and enftal
Their Moulten Gods, the Sanedrin muft fall ;

That

That Conftellation of the Jewifh Pow'r,
All blotted from its Orb muft fhine no more ;
Or ftampt in *Pharoahs* darling Mould, muft quit
Their Native Beams, for a new-model'd Light ;
Like *Egypts* Sanedrins, their influence gone,
Flafh but like empty Meteors round the Throne :
That that new Lord may *Judahs* Scepter weild,
To whom th'old Brickill Taskmafters muft yield ;
Who, to erect new Temples for his Gods,
Shall th'enflav'd *Ifrael* drive with Iron Rods ;
If they want Bricks for his new Walls t'afpire,
To their fad coft, he'll find 'em Straw and Fire.

All this t'effect, and their new Fabrick build,
Both clofe Cabals and Forreign Leagues are held :
To *Babylon* and *Egypt* they fend o're,
And both their Conduct and their Gold implore.
By fuch Abettors the fly Game was plaid ;
One of their Chiefs a Jewifh Renegade,
High-born in *Ifrael*, one *Michals* Prieft,
But now in *Babylons* proud Scarlet dreft.
'Tis to his Hands the Plotting Mandats come
Subfcrib'd by the Apoftate *Abfolom*.
Nay, and to keep themfelves all danger-proof,
That none might track the *Belial* by his Hoof,
Their Correfpondence veil'd from prying Eyes,
In Hieroglyphick Figures they difguife.
Hufht as the Night,in which their Plots combin'd,
And filent as the Graves they had defign'd,
Their Ripening Mifchiefs to perfection fprung.
But oh ! the much-loath'd *David* lives too long.
Their Vultures cannot mount but from his Tomb ;
And with too hungry ravenous Gorges come,
To be by airy Expectation fed.
No Prey, no Spoil, before they fee Him Dead.
Yes, Dead ; the Royal Sands too flowly pafs,
And therefore they're refolved to break the Glafs :
And to enfure Times tardy dubious Call,
Decree their Daggers fhould his Sythe foreftall.
For th'execrable Deed a Hireling Crew
Their Hell and They pick out ; whom to make true,

An

An Oath of Force so exquisite they frame,
Sworn in the Blood of *Israels* Paschal Lamb.
If false, the Vengeance of that Sword that slew
Egypts First-born, their perjur'd Heads pursue.
Strong was the Oath, the Imprecation dire ;
And for a Viand, lest their Guilt should tire,
With promis'd Paradice they cheer their way ;
And bold's the Souldier who has Heav'n his pay.

But the ne'r-sleeping Providence that stands
With jealous Eyes o're Truths up-lifted Hands ;
That still in its Lord *Israel* takes delight,
Their Cloud by Day, and Guardian Fire by Night ;
A Ray from out its Fiery Pillar cast,
That overlook'd their driving *Jehu's* hast.
All's ruin'd and betray'd : their own false Slaves
Detect the Plot, and dig their Masters Graves :
Not Oaths nor Bribes shall bind, when great *Jehovah* saves.
The frighted *Israelites* take the Alarm,
Resolve the Traitors Sorceries t'uncharm :
Till cursing, raving, mad, and drunk with Rage,
In *Amnons* Blood their frantick Hands engage.

Here let the Ghost of strangl'd *Amnon* come,
A Specter that will strike Amazement dumb ;
Amnon the Proto-Martyr of the Plot,
The Murder'd *Amnon*, their Eternal Blot ;
Whose too bold zeal stood like a *Pharos* Light,
Israel to warn, and track their Deeds of Night.
Till the sly Foe his unseen Game to play,
Put out the Beacon to secure his way.
Baals Cabinet-Intrigues he open spread,
The Ravisht *Tamar* for whose sake he bled.
T'unveil their Temple and expose their Gods,
Deserv'd their vengeances severest Rods :
Wrath he deserv'd, and had the Vial full,
To lay those Devils had possest his Soul.
His silenc'd Fiends from his wrung Neck they twist ;
Whilst his kind Murd'rer's but his Exorcist.
Here draw, bold Painter, (if thy Pencil dare
Unshaking write, what *Israel* quak'd to hear,)

A

A Royal Altar pregnant with a Load
Of Humane Bones beneath a Breaden God.
Altars fo rich not *Molocks* Temples fhow ;
'Twas Heaven above, and *Golgotha* below.
Yet are not all the Myftick Rites yet done :
Their pious Fury does not ftop fo foon.
But to purfue the loud-tongu'd Wounds they gave,
Refolves to ftab his Fame beyond the Grave,
And in Eternal Infamy to brand
With *Amnons* Murder, *Amnons* righteous Hand.
Here with a Bloodlefs wound, by Hellifh Art,
With his own Sword they goar his Lifelefs Heart.
Thus in a Ditch the butcher'd *Amnon* lay,
A Deed of Night enough to have kept back the Day.
Had not the Sun in Sacred vengeance rofe,
Afham'd to fee, but prouder to difclofe,
Warm'd with new Fires, with all his pofting fpeed,
Brought Heav'ns bright Lamp to fhew th'Infernal Deed.

What art thou, Church ! when Faith to propagate,
And crufh all Bars that ftop thy growing ftate,
Thou break'ft through Natures, Gods, and Humane Laws,
Whilft Murder's Merit in a Churches Caufe.
How much thy Ladder *Jacobs* does excel :
Whofe Top's in Heaven like His, but Foot in Hell ;
Thy Caufes bloody Champions to befriend,
For Fiends to Mount, as Angels to Defcend.

This was the ftroke did th'alarm'd World furprize,
And even to infidelity lent Eyes :
Whilft fweating *Abfolon* in *Ifrael* pent,
For frefher Air was to bleak *Hebron* fent.
Cold *Hebron* warm'd by his approaching fight,
Flufht with his Gold, and glow'd with new delight.
Till Sacred all-converting Intereft
To Loyalty, their almoft unknown Gueft,
Oped a broad Gate, from whence forth-iffuing come,
Decrees, Tefts, Oaths, for well-footh'd *Abfolom.*
Spight of that Guilt that made even Angels fall,
An unbarr'd Heir fhall Reign : In fpight of all
Apoftacy from Heav'n, or Natures tyes,
Though for his Throne a *Cain*-built Palace rife.

E   No

No wonder *Hebron* such Devotion bears
T'Imperial Dignity, and Royal Heirs ;
For they, whom Chronicle so high renowns
For selling Kings, should know the price of Crowns.

Here, Glorious *Hushai*, let me mourn thy Fate,
Thou once great Pillar of the *Hebron* State :
Yet now to Dungeons sent, and doom'd t'a Grave.
But Chains are no new Sufferings to the Brave.
Witness thy pains in six years Bonds endur'd,
For *Israels* Faith, and *Davids* Cause immur'd.
Death too thou oft for *Judahs* Crown hast stood,
So bravely fac'd in several Fields of Blood.
But from Fames Pinnacle now headlong cast,
Life, Honour, all are ruin'd at a Blast.
For *Absolons* great L A W thou durst explain ;
Where but to pry, bold Lord, was to prophane :
A Law that did his Mystick God-head couch,
Like th'Ark of God, and no less Death to touch.
Forgot are now thy Honourable Scars,
Thy Loyal Toyls, and Wounds in *Judahs* Wars.
Had thy pil'd Trophies *Babel*-high, reacht Heav'n,
Yet by one stroke from *Absolons* Thunder given,
Thy towring Glorie's levell'd to the ground ;
A stroke does all thy Tongues of Fame confound,
And, Traitor, now is all the Voice they sound.
True, thou hadst Law ; that even thy Foes allow ;
But to thy Advocates, as damn'd as Thou,
'Twas Death to plead it. Artless *Absolon*
The Bloody Banner to display so soon :
Such killing Beams from thy young Day-break shot ;
What will the Noon be, if the Morn's so hot?
Yes, dreadful Heir, the Coward *Hebron* awe.
So the young Lion tries his tender Paw.
At a poor Herd of feeble Heifers flies,
Ere the rough Bear, tusk'd Boar, or spotted Leopard dies.
Thus flusht, great Sir, thy strength in *Israel* try :
When their Cow'd Sanedrims shall prostrate lye,
And to thy feet their slavish Necks shall yield ;
Then raign the Princely Savage of the Field.

Yes

Yes, *Ifraels* Sanedrin, 'twas they alone
That fet too high a Value on a Throne ;
Thought they had a God was Worthy to be ferv'd ;
A Faith maintain'd, and Liberty preferv'd.
And therefore judg'd, for Safety and Renown
Of *Ifraels* People, Altars, Laws and Crown,
Th'Anointing Drops on Royal Temples fhed
Too precious Showrs for an Apoftates Head.
Then was that great Deliberate Councel giv'n,
An Act of Juftice both to Man and Heav'n,
Ifraels confpiring Foes to overthrow,
That *Abfolon* fhould th'Hopes of Crowns forego.
Debarr'd Succeffion ! oh that difmal found !
A fcand, at which *Baal* ftagger'd, and Hell groan'd ;
A found that with fuch dreadful Thunder falls,
'Twas heard even to *Semiramis* trembling Walls.

But hold ! is this the Plots laft Murd'ring Blow,
The dire divorce of Soul and Body ? No.
The mangled Snake, yet warm, to Life they'll bring,
And each disjoynted Limb together cling.
Then thus *Baals* wife confulting Prophets cheer'd
Their penfive Sons, and call'd the fcatter'd Herd.

Are we quite ruin'd ! No, miftaken Doom,
Still the great Day, yes that great Day fhall come,
(Oh, roufe our fainting Sons, and droop no more.)
A Day, whofe Lufter, our long Clouds blown o're,
Not all the Rage of *Ifrael* fhall annoy,
No, nor denouncing Sanedrims deftroy.
See yon North-Pole, and mark *Boötes Carr* :
Oh ! we have thofe Influencing Afpects there,
Thofe Friendly pow'rs that drive in that bright *Wain*,
Shall redeem All, and our loft Ground regain.
Whilft to our Glory their kind Aid ftands faft,
But one Plot more, our Greateft and our Laft.

Now for a Product of that fubtle kind,
As far above their former Births refin'd,
As Firmamental Fires t'a Tapers ray,
Or Prodigies to Natures common Clay.

Empires

Empires in Blood, or Cities in a Flame,
Are work for vulgar Hands, scarce worth a Name.
A Cake of *Shew-bread* from an Altar ta'ne,
Mixt but with some Levitical King-bane,
Has sent a Martyr'd Monarch to his Grave.
Nay, a poor Mendicant Church-Rake-hell slave
Has stab'd Crown'd Heads ; slight Work to hands well-skill'd,
Slight as the Pebble that *Goliah* kill'd.
But to make Plots no Plots, to clear all Taints,
Traitors transform to Innocents,Fiends to Saints,
Reason to Nonsence, Truth to Perjury ;
Nay, make their own attesting Records lye,
And even the gaping Wounds of Murder whole :
I this last Masterpiece requires a Soul.
Guilt to unmake, and Plots annihilate,
Is much a greater work than to create.
Nay both at once to be, and not to be,
Is such a Task would pose a Deity.
Let *Baal* do this, and be a God indeed :
Yes, t his Immortal Honour 'tis decreed,
His Sanguine Robe though dipt in reeking Gore,
With purity and Innocence all o're,
Shall dry, and spotless from the purple hue,
The Miracle of *Gideons* Fleece outdo.
Yes, they're resolv'd, in all their foes despight,
To wash their more than *Ethiop* Treason White.

But now for Heads to manage the Design,
Fit Engineers to labour in this Mine.
For their own hands 'twere fatal to employ :
Should *Baal* appear, it would *Baals* Cause destroy.
Alas, should onely their own Trumpets sound
Their Innocence, the jealous Ears around
All Infidels would the loath'd Charmer fly,
And through the Angels voice the Fiend descry.
No, this last game wants a new plotting Set,
And *Israel* only now can *Israel* cheat.
In this Machine their profest Foes must move,
Whilst *Baal* absconding sits in Clouds above,
From whence unseen he guides their bidden way :
For he may prompt, although he must not play.

This

This to effect a sort of Tools they find,
Devotion-Rovers, an Amphibious Kind,
Of no Religion, yet like Walls of Steel
Strong for the Altars where their Princes kneel.
Imperial not Celestial is their Test,
The Uppermost, indsputably Best.
They always in the golden Chariot rod,
Honour their Heav'n, and Interest their God.

Of these then subtil *Caleb* none more Great,
Caleb who shines where his lost Father set ;
Got by that sire, who not content alone,
To shade the brightest Jewel in a Crown,
Preaching Ingratitude t'a Court and Throne ;
But made his Politicks the baneful Root
From whence the springing Woes of *Israel* shoot,
When his Great Masters fatal *Gordian* tyed,
He lai'd the barren *Michal* by his side ;
That the ador'd *Absolons* immortal Line
Might on *Judeas* Throne for ever shine.
Caleb, who does that hardy Pilot make,
Steering in that Hereditary Track,
Blind to the Sea-Mark of a Fathers Wrack.

Next *Jonas* stands bull-fac'd, but chicken-soul'd,
Who once the silver Sanedrin Controul'd,
Their Gold-tip'd Tongue ; Gold his great Councels Bawd :
Till by succeeding Sanedrins outlaw'd,
He was prefer'd to guard the sacred Store :
There Lordly rowling in whole Mines of Oar ;
To Diceing Lords, a Cully-Favourite,
He prostitutes whole *Cargoes* in a Night.
Here to the Top of his Ambition come,
Fills all his Sayls for hopeful *Absolom.*
For his Religion's as the Season calls,
Gods in Possession, in Reversion *Baals.*
He bears himself a Dove to Mortal Race,
And though not Man, he can look Heav'n i'th' Face.
Never was Compound of more different Stuff,
A Heart in Lambskin, and a Conscience Buff.

Let not that Hideous Bulk of Honour scape,
Nadab that sets the gazing Crowd agape :
That old Kirk-founder, whose course Croak could sing
The Saints, the Cause, no Bishop, and no King :

F   When

When Greatnefs clear'd his Throat, and fcowr'd his Maw,
Roard out Succeffion, and the Penal Law.
Not fo of old : another found went forth,
When in the Region from *Judea* North,
By the Triumphant *Saul* he was employ'd,
A huge fang Tusk to goar poor *Davids* fide.
Like a Probofcis in the Tyrants Jaw,
To rend and root through Government and Law.
His hand that Hell-penn'd League of *Belial* drew,
That Swore down Kings, Religion overthrew,
Great *David* banifht, and Gods Prophets flew.
Nor does the Courts long Sun fo powerful fhine,
T'exhale his Vapours, or his Drofs refine ;
Nor is the Metal mended by the ftamp.
With his rank oyl he feeds the Royal Lamp.
To Sanedrins an everlafting Foe,
Refolv'd his Mighty Hunters overthrow.
And true to Tyranny, as th'only Jem,
That truly fparkles in a Diadem ;
To *Abfalons* fide does his old *Covenant* bring,
With *State* raz'd out, and interlin'd with KING.
But *Nadabs* Zeal has too fevere a Doom ;
Whilft ferving an ungrateful *Abfalom*,
His ftrength all fpent his Greatnefs to create,
He's now laid by a caft-out Drone of State.
He rowz'd that Game by which he is undone,
By fleeter Courfers now fo far outrun,
That fiercer Mightier *Nimrod* in the Chace,
Till quite thrown out, and loft he quits the Race.

Of Low-born Tools we bawling *Shimei* faw,
Jerufalems late loud-tongu'd MOUTH of Law.
By Bleffings from Almighty Bounty given,
Shimei no common Favorite of Heaven.
Whom, left Pofterity fhould loofe the Breed,
In five fhort Moons indulgent Heav'n rais'd Seed ;
Made happy in an Early teeming Bride,
And laid a lovely Heirefs by her fide.
Whilft the glad Father's fo divinely bleft,
That like the Stag proud of his Brow fo dreft,
He brandifhes his lofty City-Creft.

'Twas

'Twas in *Jerusalem* was *Shimei* nurst,
Jerusalem by *Baals* Prophets ever curst,
The greatest Block that stops 'em in their way,
For which she once in Dust and Ashes lay.
Here to the Bar this whiffling Lurcher came,
And barkt to rowze the nobler Hunters Game.
But *Shimei's* Lungs might well be stretcht so far ;
For steering by a Court-Ascendant Star,
For daily Oracles he does address,
To the *Egyptian* Beauteous Sorceress.
For *Pharoah* when he wisely did essay
To bear the long-sought Golden Prize away,
That fair Enchantress sent, whose Magick Skill
Should keep great *Israels* sleeping Dragon still.
Thus by her powerful inspirations fed,
To bite their Heels this City-Snake was bred,
Till *Absalon* got strength to bruise their Head.
Of all the Heroes since the world began,
To *Shimei Joshuah* was the bravest Man.
To Him his Tutelar Saint he prays, and oh,
That great *Jerusalem* were like *Jericoh* !
Then bellowing lowd for *Joshuahs* Spirit calls,
Because his Rams-horn blew down City-Walls.

In the same Roll have we grave *Corah* seen,
Corah, the late chief Scarlet *Abbethdin*.
Corah, who luckily i'th' Bench was got,
To loo the Bloodhounds off to save the Plot.
Corah, who once against *Baals* Impious Cause,
Stood strong for *Israels* Faith and *Davids* Laws.
He poys'd his Scales, and shook his ponderous Sword,
Lowd as his Fathers *Basan*-Bulls he roar'd ;
Till by a Dose of Forreign *Ophir* drencht,
The Feavour of his Burning Zeal was Quencht.
Ophir, that rescu'd the Court-Drugsters Fate,
Sent in the Nick to gild his Pills of State.
Whilst the' kind Skill of our Law-Emperick,
Sublim'd his Mercury to save his Neck.
In Law, they say, he had but a slender Mite,
And Sense he had less : for as Historians write,
The *Arabian* Legate laid a Snare so gay,
As Spirited his little Wits away.

Of

Of the Records of Law he fancied none
Like the Commandment Tables graved in Stone.
And wish'd the *Talmude* such, that Soveraign sway
When once displeased might th'angry *Moses* play.
Onely his Law was Brittle i'th' wrong place :
For had our *Corah* been in *Moses* Case,
The Fury of his Zeal had been employ'd
To build that Calf which th'others Rage destroy'd.
Thus *Corah*, *Baals* true Fayry Changeling made,
He Bleated onely as the *Pharisees* pray'd,
All to advance that future Tyrant pow'r,
Should Widows Houses gorge, and Orphans Tears devour.

    Nor are these all their Instruments ; to prop
Their Mighty Cause, and *Israels* Murmurs stop ;
They find a sort of Academick Tools ;
Who by the Politick Doctrine of their Schools,
Betwixt Reward, Pride, Avarice, Hope and Fear,
Prizing their Heav'n too cheap, the World too dear,
Stand bold and strong for *Absolons* Defence :
Interest the Thing, but Conscience the Pretence.
These to ensure him for their *Sions* King,
A Right Divine quite down from *Adam* bring,
That old Levitick Engine of Renown,
That makes no Taint of Souls a bar t'a Crown.
'Tis true, Religions constant Champion vow'd,
Each open-mouth'd, with Pulpit-Thunder lowd,
Against false Gods , and Idol Temples bawls ;
Yet lays the very Stones that raise their Walls.
They preach up Hell to those that *Baal* adore,
Yet make't Damnation to oppose his pow'r.
So far this Paradox of Conscience run,
Till *Israels* Faith pulls *Israels* Altars down.
Grant Heav'n they don't to *Baal* so far make way,
Those fatal *Wands* before their Sheepfolds lay.
Such Motley Principles amongst them thrown,
Shall nurse that Py-ball'd Flock that's half his own.
Nor may they say, when *Molocks* Hands draw nigher,
We built the Pile, whilst *Baal* but gives it fire.

    If Monarchy in *Adam* first begun,
When the Worlds Monarch dug, and his Queen spun,

                       And

His Fig-leaves his firſt Coronation-Robe,
His Spade his Scepter, and her Wheel his Globe ;
And Royal Birthright, as their Schools aſſert,
Not Kings themſelves with Conſcience can divert ;
How came the World poſſeſt by *Adams* Sons,
Such various Principalities, Powres, Thrones ?
When each went out and choſe what Lands he pleas'd,
Whilſt a new Family new Kingdoms rais'd ?
His Sons aſſuming what he could not give,
Their Soveraign Sires right Heir they did deprive ;
And from Rebellion all their pow'r derive :
For were there an original Majeſty
Upheld by Right Divine, the World ſhould be
Onely one Univerſal Monarchy.
O cruel Right Divine, more full of Fate,
Then th' Angels flaming Sword at *Edens* Gate,
Such early Treaſon through Mankind convey'd,
And at the door of Infant-Nature layd.
For Right Divine in *Eſau's* juſt defence,
Why don't they quarrel with Omnipotence,
The firſt-born *Eſau's* Right to *Jacob* giv'n,
And Gods gift too, Injuſtice charge on Heav'n.
Nay, let Heav'n anſwer this one Fact alone,
Mounting a Baſtard *Jephtha* on a Throne.
If Kings and Sanedrims thoſe Laws could make,
Which from offending Heirs their Heads can take ;
And a Firſt-born can forfeit Life and Throne,
And all by Law : why not a Crown alone ?
Strange-bounded Law-makers ! whoſe pow'r can throw
The deadlier Bolt, can't give the weaker Blow.
A Treaſonous Act ; nay, but a Treaſonous Breath
Againſt offended Majeſty is Death.
But, oh ! the wondrous Church-diſtinction given
Between the Majeſty of Kings and Heav'n !
The venial ſinner here, he that intreagues
With *Egypt*, *Babylon* ; Cabals, Plots, Leagues
With *Iſraels* Foes her Altars to deſtroy,
A Hair untouch'd, ſhall Health, Peace, Crowns enjoy.

Truths Temple thus the Exhalations bred
From her own Bowels, to obſcure her Head.

G   And

And *Abſolom* already had ſubdu'd
Whole Crowds of the unthinking Multitude.
But through theſe Wiles too weak to catch the Wiſe,
Thin as their Ephod-Lawn, a Cobweb Net for Flyes,
The ſearching Sanedrim ſaw ; and to diſpel
Th'ingendring Miſts that threatned *Iſrael*,
They ſtill reſolv'd their Plotting Foes defeat,
By barring *Abſolon* th'Imperial Seat.

But here's his greateſt Tug ; could he but make
Th'encluding Sanedrims Reſolves once ſhake ;
Nay, make the ſmalleſt Breach, or claſhing Jar,
In their great Councel, puſh but home ſo far,
And the great Point's ſecur'd.----And, lo! among
The Princely Heads of that Illuſtrious Throng,
He ſaw rich Veins with Noble Blood new fill'd ;
Others who Honour from Dependance held.
Some with exhauſted Fortunes, to ſupport
Their Greatneſs, propt with Crutches from a Court.
Theſe for their Countries Right their Votes ſtill paſs,
Mov'd like the Water in a Weather-glaſs,
Higher or lower, as the powerful Charm
O'th' Soveraign Hand is either cool or warm.
Here muſt th'Attacque be made : for well we know,
Reaſon and Titles from one Fountain flow :
Whilſt Favour Men no leſs than Fortunes builds,
And Honour ever Moulds as well as Guilds.
Honour that ſtill does even new Souls inſpire ;
Honour more powerful than the Heav'n-ſtoln Fire.
Theſe muſt be wrought to *Abſolons* Defence.
For though to baffle the whole Sanedrims Sence,
T'attempt Impoſſibles would be in vain,
Yet 'tis enough but to *Divide* and *Raign*.

Here though ſmall Force ſuch eaſie Converts draws,
Yet 'tis thought fit in glory to their Cauſe,
Some learned Champion of prodigious Senſe,
With Mighty and long ſtudyed Eloquence,
Should with a kind of Inſpiration riſe,
And the unguarded Sanedrim ſurprize,
And ſuch reſiſtleſs conquering Reaſons preſs,
To charm their vanquiſht Souls, that the Succeſs   }
Might look like Conſcience, though 'tis nothing leſs. }   For

For this Defign no Head nor Tongue fo well,
As that of the profound *Achitophel.*
How, great *Achitophel* ! his Hand, his Tongue !
Babylons Mortal Foe ; he who fo long
With haughty Sullennefs, and fcornful Lowr,
Had loath'd falfe Gods, and Arbitrary pow'r.
'Gainft *Baal* no Combatant more fierce than he ;
For *Ifraels* afferted Liberty,
No Man more bold ; with generous Rage enflam'd,
Againft the old enfnaring Teft declaim'd.
Befide, he bore a moft peculiar Hate
To fleeping Pilots, all Earth-clods of State.
None more abhorr'd the Sycophant Buffoon,
And Parafite, th'excrefcence of a Throne ;
Creatures who their creating Sun difgrace,
A Brood more abject than *Niles* Slime-born Race.
Such was the Brave *Achitophel* ; a Mind,
(If but the Heart and Face were of a kind)
So far from being by one bafe Thought deprav'd,
That fure half ten fuch Souls had *Sodom* fav'd.
Here *Baals* Cabal *Achitophel* furvey'd,
And dafht with wonder, half defpairing faid,
Is this the Hand that *Abfolon* muft Crown,
The Founder of his Temples, Palace, Throne ?
This, This the mighty Convert we muft make ?
Gods, h'has a Soul not all our Arts can fhake.

At this a nicer graver Head ftept out,
And with this Language chid their groundlefs Doubt :
For fhame, no more ; what is't that frights you thus ?
Is it his Hatred of our God, and us,
Makes him fo formidable in your Eye ?
Or is't his Wit, Senfe, Honour, Bravery ?
Give him a thoufand Virtues more, and plant
Them round him like a Wall of Adamant,
Strong as the Gates of Heaven ; we'll reach his Heart :
Cheer, cheer, my Friends, I've found one Mortal part.
For he has *Pride,* a vaft infatiate *Pride,*
Kind Stark, he's vulnerable on that fide.
Pride that made Angels fall, and pride that hurl'd
Entayl'd Deftruction through a ruin'd World.

Adam

Adam from Pride to Disobedience ran :
To be like Gods, made a lost wretched Man.
There, there, my Sons, let our pour'd strength all fly :
For some bold Tempter now to rap him high,
From Pinnacles to Mountain Tops, and show
The gaudy Glories of the World below.

At which the Consult came to this Design,
To work him by a kind of Touch Divine.
To raise some holy Spright to do the Feat.
Nothing like Dreams and Visions to the Great.
Did not a little Witch of *Endor* bring
A Visionary Seer t'a cheated King ?
And shall their greater Magick want Success,
Their more Illustrious Sorceries do less !

This final Resolution made, at last
Some Mystick words, and invocations past,
They call'd the Spirit of a late Court-Scribe ;
Once a true Servant of the Plotting Tribe :
When both with Forreign and Domestick Cost,
He plaid the feasted Sanedrims kind Host.
H'had scribbled much, and like a Patriot bold,
Bid high for *Israels* Peace with *Egypts* Gold.
But since a Martyr. (Why ! as Writers think,
His Masters Hand had over-gall'd his Ink.)
And by protesting *Absoloms* wise care,
Popt into Brimstone ere he was aware.
Him from the Grave they rais'd, in ample kind,
His sever'd Head to his seer Quarters joyn'd ;
Then cas'd his Chin in a false Beard so well,
As made him pass for Father *Samuel.*
Him thus equipt in a Religious Cloak,
They thus his new-made Reverence bespoke.

Go, awful Spright, hast to *Achitophel,*
Rouze his great Soul, use every Art, Charm, Spell :
For *Absolom* thy utmost Rhetorick try,
Preach him Succession, roar'd Succession cry,
Succession drest in all her glorious pride,
Succession Worshipt, Sainted, Deify'd.

Conjure

Conjure him by Divine and Humane Pow'rs,
Convince, Convert, Confound, make him but ours,
That *Abfolon* may mount on *Judahs* Throne,
Whilft all the World before us is our own.

The forward Spright but few Inftructions lackt,
Strait by the Moons pale light away he packt,
And in a trice, his Curtains open'd wide,
He fate him by *Achitophels* Bed-fide.
And in this ftyle his artful Accents ran.

Hear *Ifraels* Hope, thou more than happy Man,
Beloved on high, witnefs this Honour done
By Father S...muel, and believe me, Son,
'Tis by no common Mandate of a God,
A Soul beatifyed, the bleft Abode
Thus low deferting, quits Immortal Thrones,
And from his Grave refumes his fleeping Bones.
But Heavn's the Guide, and wondrous is the way,
Divine the Embaffie : hear, and obey.
How long, *Achitophel*, and how profound
A Mift of Hell has thy loft Reafon drown'd ?
Can the Apoftacy from *Ifraels* Faith,
In *Ifraels* Heir, deferve a murmuring Breath ?
Or to preferve Religion, Liberty,
Peace, Nations, Souls, is that a Caufe fo high,
As the Right Heir from Empire to debar ?
Forbid it Heav'n, and guard him every Star.
Alas, what if an Heir of Royal Race,
Gods Glory and his Temples will deface,
And make a prey of your Eftates, Lives, Laws ;
Nay, give your Sons to *Molocks* burning paws ;
Shall you exclude him ? hold that Impious Hand.
As *Abraham* gave his Son at Gods Command,
Think ftill he does by *Divine Right* fucceed :
God bids Him Reign, and you fhould bid Them Bleed.
'Tis true, as Heav'ns Elected Flock, you may
For his Converfion, and your Safety *pray*
But Pray'rs are all. To Difinherit him,
The very Thought, nay, Word it felf's a Crime.
For that's the MEANS of Safety : but forbear,
For Means are Impious in the Sons of Pray'r.

H   To

To Miracles alone your Safety owe ;
And *Abrahams* Angel wait to ſtop the Blow.
Yes, what if his polluted Throne be ſtrowd
With Sacriledge, Idolatry, and Blood ;
And 'tis you mount him there ; you're innocent ſtill :
For he's a King, and Kings can do no ill.
Oh Royal Birthright, 'tis a Sacred Name :
Rowze then *Achitophel*, rowze up for ſhame :
Let not this Lethargy thy Soul benum ;
But wake, and ſave the Godlike *Abſolom*.
And to reward thee for a Deed ſo great
Glut thy Deſires, thy full-crown'd wiſhes meet,
Be with accumulated Honours bleſt,
And graſp a S T A R t'adorn thy ſhining Creſt.

Achitophel before his Eyes could ope,
Dreamt of an Ephod, Mitre, and a Cope.
Thoſe viſionary Robes t'his Eyes appear'd :
For Prieſtly all was the great Senſe he heard.
But Prieſt or Prophet, Right Divine, or all
Together ; 'twas not at their feebler call,
'Twas at the *Star* he wak'd ; the *Star* but nam'd,
Flaſht in his Eyes, and his rowz'd Soul enflam'd.
A *Star*, whoſe Influence had more powerful Light,
Then that Miraculous Wanderer of the Night,
Decreed to guide the Eaſtern Sages way :
Their's to adore a God, his to betray.

Here the new Convert more than half inſpir'd,
Strait to his Cloſet and his Books retir'd.
There for all needful Arts in this extreme,
For knotty Sophiſtry t'a limber Theme,
Long brooding ere the Maſs to Shape was brought,
And after many a tugging heaving Thought,
Together a well-orderd Speech he draws,
With ponderous Sounds for his much-labour'd Cauſe.
Then the aſtoniſht Sanedrim he ſtorm'd,
And with ſuch doughty ſtrength the Tug perform'd :
Fate did the Work with ſo much Conqueſt bleſs,
Wondrous the Champion, Glorious the Succeſs.
So powerful Eloquence, ſo ſtrong was Wit ;
And with ſuch Force the eaſie Wind-falls hit.

But

But the entireſt Hearts his Cauſe could ſteal,
Were the Levitick Chiefs of *Iſrael*.
None with more Rage the Impious Thought run down
Of barring *Abſolon*, Pow'r, Wiſhes, Crown.
With ſo much vehemence, ſuch fiery Zeal !
Oh, poor unhappy Church of *Iſrael !*
Thou feelſt the Fate of the Arch-angels Wars,
The Dragons Tayl ſweeps down thy Falling Stars.
Nay, the black Vote 'gainſt *Abſolon* appear'd
So monſtrous, that they damn'd it ere 'twas heard.
For Prelates ne'r in Sanedrims debate,
They argue in the Church, but not i'th' State ;
And when their Thoughts aſlant towards Heav'n they turn,
They weigh each Grain of Incenſe that they burn,
But t'Heavens Vice-gerents, Soul, Senſe, Reaſon, all,
Or right or wrong, like Hecatombs muſt fall.
And when State-buſineſs calls their Thoughts below,
Then like their own Church-Organ-Pipes they go.
Not *Davids* Lyre could more his Touch obey :
For as their Princes breathe and ſtrike, they play.
'Gainſt Royal Will they never can diſpute,
But by a ſtrange *Tarantula* ſtrook mute, }
Dance to no other Tune but *Abſolute*.
All Acts of Supreme Power they ſtill admire :
'Tis Sacred, though to ſet the World on Fire,
Though Church-Infallibility they explode,
As making Humane knowledge equal God ;
Infallible in a new name goes down,
Not in the Mitre lodged, but in the Crown.
'Tis true, bleſt *Deborahs* Laws they could forget :
(But want of Memory commends their Wit.)
Where 'twas enacted Treaſon, not to own
Hers and her Sanedrins right to place the Crown.
But her weak Heads oth' Church, miſtaken fools,
Wanted the Light of their ſublimer Schools :
For Divine Right could no ſuch Forces bring.
But Wiſdom now expands her wider Wing, }
And Streams are ever deeper than the Spring.
Beſides, they've ſenſe of Honour ; and who knows
How far the Gratitude of Prieſt-craft goes ?

                                        And

And what if now like old *Elisha* fed,
To praise the Sooty Bird that brought 'em Bread,
In pure acknowledgment, though in despight
Of their own sense, they paint the Raven White.

Achitophel charm'd with kind Fortunes Smiles,
Flusht with Success, now glows for bolder Toyls.
Great Wits perverted greatest Mischiefs hold,
As poysonous Vapors spring from Mines of Gold.
And proud to see himself with Triumph blest,
Thus to great *Absolom* himself addrest.

Illustrious Terrour of the World, all hayle :
For ever like your Conquering Self prevaile.
In spight of Malice in full Luster shine ;
Be your each Action, Word, and Look Divine.
Nay, though our Altars you've so long forborne ;
To your derided Foes Defeat, and Scorne,
For your Renown we have those Trumpets found,
Shall ev'n this Deed your highest Glory sound.
That spight of the ill-judging Worlds mistake,
Your Soul still owns those Temples you forsake :
Onely by all-commanding Honour driven,
This self-denial you have made with Heav'n :
Quitting our Altars, cause the Insolence
Of prophane Sanedrims has driven you thence.
A Prince his Faith to such low Slaves reveal !
'Twas Treason though to God to bid You kneel.
And what though senseless barking Murmurers scold, ⎫
And with a Rage too blasphemously bold,   ⎬
Say *Israels* Crown 's for *Esau*'s Pottage sold. ⎭
Let 'em rayl on ; and to strike Envy dumb ;
May the Slaves live till that great Day shall come,
When their husht Rage shall your keen Vengeance fly,
And silenc'd with your Royal Thunder dye.
Nay, to outsoar your weak Fore-fathers Wings,
And to be all that Nature first meant Kings ;
Damn'd be the Law that Majesty confines,
But doubly damn'd accursed Sanedrins,
Invented onely to eclipse a Crown.
Oh throw that dull Mosaick Land-mark down.

The

The making Sanedrims a part of Pow'r,
Nurst but those Vipers which its Sire devour.
Lodg'd in the Pallace tow'rds the Throne they press,
For Pow'rs Enjoyment does its Lust increase.
Allegiance onely is in Chains held fast;
Make Men ne're thirst, is ne're to let 'em tast.
Then, Royal Sir, be Sanedrims no more,
Lop off that rank Luxurious Branch of pow'r :
Those hungry *Scions* from the *Cedar* root,
That its Imperial Head towards Heav'n may shoot.
When Lordly Sanedrims with Kings give Law,
And thus in yokes like Mules together draw ;
From *Judahs* Arms the Royal Lyon raze,
And *Iffachars* dull Ass supply the place.
If Kings o're common Mankind have this odds,
Are Gods Vicegerents; let 'em act like Gods.
As Man is Heav'ns own clay, which it may mould
For Honour or Dishonour, uncontrould,
And Monarchy is mov'd by Heav'nly Springs ;
Why is not Humane Fate i'th' Breath of Kings ?
Then, Sir, from Heav'n your great Example take,
And be th'unbounded Lord a King should make :
Resume what bold Invading Slaves engrost,
And onely Pow'rs Effeminacy lost.

      To this kind *Absolom* but little spoke ;
Onely return'd a Nod, and gracious Look.
For though recorded Fame with pride has told,
Of his great Actings, Wonders manifold ;
And his great Thinkings most Diviners guess ;
Yet his great Speakings no Records express.

      All things thus safe ; and now for one last blow,
To give his Foes a total Overthrow ;
A Blow not in Hells Legends match'd before,
The remov'd Plot's laid at the Enemies door.
The old Plot forg'd against the Saints of *Baal*,
Cheat, Perjury, and Subornation all,
Whilst with a more damn'd Treason of their own,
Like working Moles they're digging round the Throne ;
Baal, *Baal*, the cry, and *Absolom* the Name,
But *Davids* glory, Life and Crown the Aim.

I   Nay,

Nay, if but a Petition peep abroad,
Though for the Glory both of Church and God,
And to preserve even their yet unborn Heirs ;
There's Blood and Treason in their very Prayers.
This unexampled Impudence upheld ;
The Governments best Friends, the Crowns best Sheild,
The Great and Brave with equal Treason brands.
Faith, Honour, and Allegiance strongest Bands
All broken like the Cords of *Sampson* fall,
Whilst th' universal Leprosie taints all.
These poysonous shafts with greater spleen they draw,
Than the Outragious Wife of *Potypha.*
So the chast *Joseph* unseduc'd to her
Adult'ries, was pronounc'd a Ravisher.

This hellish Ethnick Plot the Court alarms ;
The Traytors seventy thousand strong in Arms,
Near *Endor* Town lay ready at a Call,
And garrison'd in Airy Castles all.
These Warriours on a sort of Coursers rid,
Ne'r log'd in Stables, or by Man bestrid.
What though the steele with which the Rebels fought,
No Forge e're felt, or Anvile ever wrought ?
Yet this Magnetick Plot, for black Designs,
Can raise cold Iron from the very Mines.
To this were twenty Under-plots, contriv'd
By Malice, and by Ignorance believ'd,
Till Shamms met Shamms, and Plots with Plots so crost,
That the True Plot amongst the False was lost.

Of all the much-wrong'd Worthies of the Land
Whom this Contagious Infamy profan'd,
In the first Rank the youthful *Ithream* stood,
His Princely Veins fill'd with great *Davids* Blood.
With so much Manly Beauty in his Face,
Scarce his High Birth could lend a Nobler Grace.
And for a Mind fit for this shrine of Gold
Heaven cast his Soul in the same Beauteous Mould ;
With all the sweets of Prideless Greatness blest,
As Affable as *Abrahams* Angel-Guest.
But when in Wars his glittering Steel he drew,
No Chief more Bold with fiercer Lightning flew:

Witness

Witneſs his tryal of an Arm Divine,
Paſſing the Ordeal of a *Burning Mine* :
Such forward Courage did his Boſome fill,
Starting from nothing, but from doing ill.
Still with ſuch Heat in Honours Race he run,
Such Wonders by his early Valour done,
Enough to charm a ſecond *Joſhua's* Sun.
But he has Foes ; his ſatal Enemies
To a ſtrange Monſter his Fair Truth diſguiſe ;
And ſhew the Gorgon even to Royal Eyes.
To their falſe perſpectives his Fate he owes,
The ſpots i'th' Glaſs, not in the Star it ſhows.
Yet when by the Imperial Sentence doom'd,
The Royal Hand the Princely Youth unplum'd,
He his hard Fate without a Murmur took,
And ſtood with that Calm, Duteous, Humble look.
Of all his ſhining Honours unarray'd,
Like *Iſaac's* Head on *Abrahams* Altar lay'd.
Yes, *Abſolom*, thou haſt him in the Toyl,
Rifled, and loſt ; now Triumph in the Spoyl.
His Zeal too high for *Iſraels* Temples ſoar'd,
His God-like Youth by proſtrate Hearts ador'd,
Till thy Revenge from Spight and Fear began,
And too near Heaven took Care to make him Man.
Though *Iſraels* King, God, Laws, ſhare all his Soul,
Adorn'd with all that Heroes can enrol,
Yet Vow'd Succeſſions cruel Sacrifice,
Great *Judah's* Son like *Jeptha's* Daughter dies.
Yes, like a Monument of Wrath he ſtands ;
Such Ruine *Abſolons* Revenge demands ;
His Curioſity his Doom aſſign'd :
For 'twas a Crime of as deſtructive Kind,
To pry how *Babylons* Burning Zeal aſpires,
As to look back on Sodoms blazing Fires.
But ſpoyl'd, and rob'd, his droſſier Glories gone,
His Virtue and his Truth are ſtill his own.
No rifling Hands can that bright Treaſure take,
Nor all his Foes that Royal Charter ſhake.

The dreadful'ſt Foe their Engines muſt ſubdue,
The ſtrongeſt Rock through which their Arts muſt hew,
Was great *Barzillai* : could they reach his Head,
Their Fears all huſht, they had ſtrook Danger dead.

That

That second *Moses-Guide* resolv'd to free
Our *Israel* from her threatning Slavery,
Idolatry and Chains; both from the Rods
Of *Pharoh*-Masters, and *Egyptian* Gods:
And from that Wilderness of Errour freed,
Where Dogstars scorch, and killing Serpents breed:
That *Israels* Liberty and Truth may grow,
The *Canaan* whence our Milk and Honey flow.
Such our *Barzillai*; but *Barzillai* too,
With *Moses* Fate does *Moses* Zeal pursue:
Leads to that Bliss which his own Silver Hairs
Shall never reach, Rich onely to his Heirs.
Kind Patriot, who to plant us Banks of Flow'rs,
With purling Streams, cool Shades, and Summer Bow'rs,
His Ages needful Rest away does fling,
Exhausts his Autumn to adorn our Spring:
Whilst his last hours in Toyls and Storms are hurl'd,
And onely to enrich th'inheriting World.
Thus prodigally throws his Lifes short span,
To play his Countries generous Pelican.
But oh, that all-be-devill'd Paper, fram'd,
No doubt, in Hell; that Mass of Treason damn'd;
By *Esau's* Hands, and *Jacobs* Voice disclos'd;
And timely to th' Abhorring World expos'd.
Nay, what's more wondrous, this wast-paper Tool,
A nameless, unsubscrib'd, and useless scrowl,
Was, by a Politician great in Fame,
(His Chains foreseen a Month before they came)
Preserv'd on purpose, by his prudent care,
To brand his Soul, and ev'n his Life ensnare.
But then the Geshuritish Troop, well-Oath'd,
And for the sprucer Face, well-fed, and Cloath'd.
These to the Bar Obedient Swearers go,
With all the Wind their manag'd Lungs can blow.
So have I seen from Bellows brazen Snout,
The Breath drawn in, and by th'same Hand squeez'd out.
But helping Oaths may innocently fly,
When in a Faith where dying Vows can lye.
Were Treason and Democracie his Ends,
Why was't not prov'd by his Revolting Friends?
Why did not th'Oaths of his once-great Colleagues,
Achitophel and the rest prove his Intreagues?

Why

Why at the Bar appear'd such sordid scum,
And all those Nobler Tongues of Honour dumb?
Could he his Plots this great Allies conceal,
He durst to leaky Starving Wretches tell;
Such Ignorant Princes, and such knowing Slaves;
His *Babel* building Tools from such poor Knaves.
Were he that Monster his new Foes would make
Th'unreasoning World beleive, his Soul so black,
That they in Conscience did his Side forego,
Knowing him guilty they could prove him so.
Then 'twas not Conscience made 'em change their side.
Or if they knew, yet did his Treasons hide;
In not exposing his detested Crime,
They're greater Monsters than they dare think Him.
Are these the Proselites renown'd so high,
Converta to Duty, Honour, Loyalty?
Poorly they change, who in their change stand mute:
Converts to Truth ought Falsehood to confute.
To conquering Truth, they but small glory give,
Who turn to God, yet let the Dagon live.

But who can *Amiels* charming Wit withstand,
The great State-pillar of the Muses Land.
For lawless and ungovern'd, had the Age
The Nine wild Sisters seen run mad with Rage,
Debaucht to Savages, till his keen Pen
Brought their long banisht Reason back again,
Driven by his Satyres into Natures Fence,
And lasht the idle Rovers into Sense.
Nay, his sly Muse, in Style Prophetick, wrot
The whole Intrigue of *Israels* Ethnick Plot;
Form'd strange Battalions, in stupendious-wise,
Whole Camps in Masquerade, and Armies in disguise.
Amiel, whose generous Gallantry, whilst Fame
Shall have a Tongue, shall never want a Name.
Who, whilst his Pomp his lavish Gold consum's,
Moulted his Wings to lend a Throne his Plumes,
Whilst an Ungrateful Court he did attend,
Too poor to pay, what it had pride to spend.

But, *Amiel* has, alas, the fate to hear,
An angry Poet play his Chronicler;

K   A

A Poet rais'd above Oblivions Shade,
By his Recorded Verse Immortal made.
But, Sir, his livelier Figure to engrave,
With Branches added to the *Bays* you gave:
No Muse could more Heroick Feats rehearse,
Had with an equal all-applauding Verse,
Great *Davids* Scepter, and *Sauls* Javelin prais'd :
A Pyramide to his Saint, *Interest*, rais'd.
For which Religiously no Change he mist,
From Common-wealths-man up to Royalist :
Nay, would have been his own loath'd thing call'd *Priest*.
Priest, whom with so much Gall he does describe,
'Cause once unworthy thought of *Levies* Tribe.
Near those bright Tow'rs where Art has Wonders done,
Where *Davids* fight glads the blest Summers Sun ;
And at his feet proud *Jordans* Waters run ;
A Cell there stands by Pious Founders rais'd,
Both for its Wealth and Learned *Rabbins* prais'd :
To this did an Ambitious Bard aspire,
To be no less than Lord of that blest Quire :
Till Wisdom deem'd so Sacred a Command,
A Prize too great for his unhallow'd Hand.
Besides, lewd Fame had told his plighted Vow,
To *Laura's* cooing Love percht on a dropping Bough
Laura in faithful Constancy confin'd
To *Ethiops* Envoy, and to all Mankind.
Laura though Rotten, yet of Mold Divine ;
He had all her Cl--ps, and She had all his Coine.
Her Wit so far his Purse and Sense could drain,
Till every P--x was sweetn'd to a Strain.
And if at last his Nature can reform,
A weary grown of Loves tumultuous storm,
'Tis Ages Fault, not His ; of pow'r bereft,
He left not Whoring, but of that was left.

But wandring Muse bear up thy flagging Wing :
To thy more glorious Theme return, and sing
Brave *Jothams* Worth, Impartial, Great, and Just,
Of unbrib'd Faith, and of unshaken Trust :
Once *Geshurs* Lord, their Throne so nobly fill'd,
As if to th'borrow'd Scepter that he held,

Th'in-

Th'infpiring *David* yet more generous grew,
And lent him his Imperial *Genius* too.
Nor has he worn the Royal Image more
In *Ifraels* Viceroy, than Embaffador :
Witnefs his Gallantry that refolute hour,
When to uphold the Sacred Pride of Pow'r,
His ftubborn Flags from the *Sydonian* fhore,
The angry ftorms of Thundring Caftles bore.
But thefe are Virtues Fame muft lefs admire,
Becaufe deriv'd from that Heroick Sire,
Who on a Block a dauntlefs Martyr dy'd,
With all the Sweetnefs of a Smiling Bride ;
Charm'd with the Thought of Honours Starry Pole,
With Joy laid down a Head to mount a Soul.

Of all the Champions rich in Honours Scarrs,
Whofe Loyalty through *Davids* ancient Wars,
(In fpight of the triumphant Tyrants pride,)
Was to his loweft Ebb of Fortune ty'd ;
No Link more ftrong in all that Chain of Gold,
Then *Amafai*, the Conftant, and the Bold.
That Warlike General whofe avenging Sword,
Through all the Battles of his Royal Lord,
Pour'd all the Fires that Loyal Zeal could light,
No brighter Star in the loft *Davids* night.

No lefs with Laurels *Afhurs* Brows adorn,
That mangled Brave who with *Tyres* Thunder torn,
Brought a difmember'd Load of Honour home,
And lives to make both th'Earth and Seas his Tomb.

With Reverence the Religious *Helon* treat,
Refin'd from all the loofenefs of the Great.
Helon who fees his Line of Virtues run
Beyond the Center of his Grave, his own
Unfinifht Lufter fparkling in his Son.
A Son fo high in Sanedrims renown'd,
In *Ifraels* Intreft ftrong, in Senfe profound.
Under one Roof here Truth a Goddefs dwells,
The Pious Father builds her Shrines and Cells,
And in the Son fhe fpeaks her Oracles.

In the fame lift young *Adriels* praife record,
Adriel the Academick Neighbour Lord ;
Adriel ennobled by a Grandfather,
And Unkle, both thofe Glorious Sons of War :
Both Generals, and both Exiles with their Lord ;
Till with the Royal Wanderer reftored,
They lived to fee his Coronation Pride ;
Then furfeiting on too much Tranfport dy'd.
O're *Adriels* Head thefe Heroes Spirits fhine,
His Soul with fo much Loyal Blood fenc'd in ;
Such Native Virtues his great Mind adorn,
Whilft under their congenial Influence born.

In this Record let *Camries* Name appear,
The Great *Barzillai's* Fellow Sufferer ;
From unknown Hands, of unknown Crimes accus'd,
Till th'hunted Shadow loft, his Chains unloos'd.

Now to the Sweet-tongu'd *Amrams* praife be juft,
Once the *State-Advocate*, that Wealthy Truft,
Till Flattery the price of dear-bought Gold,
His Innocence for Pallaces unfold,
To Naked Truths more fhining Beauties true,
Th'Embroider'd Mantle from his Neck he threw.

Next *Hothriel* write, *Baals* watchful Foe, and late
Jerufalems protecting Magiftrate ;
Who, when falfe Jurors were to Frenzy Charm'd,
And againft Innocence even Tribunals arm'd,
Saw deprav'd Juftice ope her Ravenous Jaw,
And timely broke her Canine Teeth of Law.

Amongft th'Afferters of his Countries Caufe,
Give the bold *Micah* his deferv'd Applaufe,
The Grateful Sanedrims repeated Choice,
Of Two Great Councels the Succeffive Voice.
Of that old hardy Tribe of *Ifrael* borne,
Fear their Difdain, and Flattery their Scorne,
Too proud to truckle, and too Tough to bend.

Of the fame Tribe was *Hanan*, *Ithreams* Friend,
From that fam'd Sire, the Long Robes Glory, fprung,
In Sanedrims his Countries Pillar long ;

Long

Long had he fadom'd all the Depths of State ;
Could with that ftrength, that ponderous Senfe debate, }
As turn'd the Scale of Nations with the weight :
Till fubtley made by Spightful Honour Great,
Prefer'd to *Ifraels* Chief Tribunal Seat,
Made in a higher Orb his Beams difpenfe,
To hufh his Formidable Eloquence.

But *Ifraels* numerous Worthies are too long
And Great a Theam for one continued Song.
Yet Thefe by bold flagitious Tongues run down,
Made all Confpirers againft *Davids* Crown.

Nay, and there was a Time, had Hell prevail'd,
Nor Perjury and Subornation fail'd,
When a long Lift of Names, for Treafon doom'd,
Had *Ifraels* Patriots in one Grave entomb'd :
A Lift, with fuch fair Loyal Colours laid,
Even to no lefs than Royal Hands convey'd.
And the great Mover in this pious Fraud,
A Dungeon Slave redeem'd by a Midnight Bawd :
Then made by Art a Swearer of Renown,
Nurft and embrac'd by th'Heir of *Judahs* Crown :
Encourag'd too by Penfion for Reward,
With his forg'd Scrowls for Guiltlefs Blood prepar'd.
Poor Engine for a greatnefs fo fublime :
But oh, a Caufe by which their *Baal* muft climb, }
Ennobles both the Actor and the Crime.

Yet This, and all Things elfe now quite blown o're,
And *Abfolom*, his *Ifraels* Fear no more :
Lufter and Pride fhall hem his radiant Brow ;
All Knees fhall fall, and proftrate Nations bow.
By Heav'ns, he is, he will, he muft, he fhall
Be *Ifraels* Heroe, Friend, Saint, Idol, all.
What though provok'd with all the crying fins
Of Murmuring Slaves, excluding Sanedrins :
By profane Crowds in dirt his Prophets fpurn d,
And ev'n his Gods in mock Proceffions burn'd :
Himfelf from *Ifrael* into *Hebron* fent,
And doom'd to little lefs than Banifhment.

In fpight of all his Scrowls to *Babylon* ;
And all the promis'd Wonders to be done,
When *Egypts* Frogs fhould croak on *Judahs* Throne.
Though of a Faith that propagates in Blood ;
Of Paffions unforgiving, lefs withftood
Then Seas and Tempefts, and as Deaf as they.
Yet all Divine fhall be his Godlike Sway,
And his calm Reign but one long *Halcyon* Day.
And this Great Truth he's damn'd that dares deny ;
'Gainft *Abfolom* even Oracles would lye,
Though Senfe and Reafon Preach 'tis Blafphemy.
Then let our dull Miftaken Terrour ceafe,
When even our Comets fpeak all Health and Peace.

F I N I S.

E R R A T A.

THE Reader is defired to Correct thefe following Miftakes. Page 1. line 12. for *Hold*, read *Hold*. p. 4. l. 22. r. *Ships* ; ibid. l. 26. for *Kindf*d, r. *Rank'd* ; ibid. l. 32. r. *the Mighty* ; ibid. l. 37. for they r. thus ; p. 7. l. 18. for *poor*, r. *weak* ; p. 9. l. 3. & 4. for his r. a ; l. 6. for *the*, r. *ye* ; ibid. l. 20. r. *Walls* ; the Billows pour ; p. 12. l. 12. r. *Arv'd ftrait* ; p. 13. l. 37. for *be* r. *take* p.32.l.10.r.*Excluding*.

Poetical Reflections

ON A LATE

POEM

ENTITULED,

Abſalom and Achitophel.

By a Perſon of Honour.

LONDON:

Printed for *Richard Janeway.* 1681.

TO THE
READER.

IF ever any thing, call'd a *Poem*, deserv'd a severe
Reflection, that of *Abſalom* and *Achitophel* may
juſtly contract it.   For tho' Lines can never be
purg'd from the droſs and filth they would throw on
others (there being no retraction that can expiate the
conveying of perſons to an unjuſt and publick re-
proach); yet the cleanſing of their fames from a deſign'd pollution, may well become a more ingenious
Pen than the Author of theſe few reflections will pre-
ſume to challenge.

To epitomize which ſcandalous Phamphlet (unworthy the denomination of *Poeſy*) no eye can in-
ſpect it without a prodigious amazement; the abuſes
being ſo groſs and deliberate, that it ſeems rather a
Capital or National Libel, than perſonal expoſures,
in order to an infamous detraction.   For how does
he character the King, but as a broad figure of ſcandalous inclinations, or contriv'd unto ſuch irregula-
rities, as renders him rather the property of Para-
ſites and Vice, than ſuitable to the accompliſhment
of ſo excellent a Prince? Nay, he forces on King
David ſuch a Royal reſemblance, that he darkens

B

his

his sanctity in spite of illuminations from Holy Writ.

Next (to take as near our King as he could) he calumniates the Duke of *Monmouth* with that height of impudence, that his Sense is far blacker than his Ink, exposing him to all the censures that a Murderer, a Traytor, or what a Subject of most ambitious evil can possibly comprehend: and it is some wonder, that his Lines also had not hang'd him on a Tree, to make the intended *Absalom* more compleat.

As to my Lord *Shaftsbury* (in his collusive *Achitophel*), what does he other than exceed Malice it self? or that the more prudent deserts of that Peer were to be so impeach'd before hand by his impious Poem, as that he might be granted more emphatically condign of the Hangman's Ax; And which his Muse does in effect take upon her to hasten.

And if the season be well observ'd, when this Adulterate Poem was spread, it will be found purposely divulg'd near the time when this Lord, with his other Noble Partner, were to be brought to their Tryals. And I suppose this Poet thought himself enough assur'd of their condemnation; at least, that his *Genius* had not otherwise ventur'd to have trampled on persons of such eminent Abilities, and Interest in the Nation. A consideration, I confess, incited my Pen (its preceding respect being paid to the Duke of *Monmouth*) to vindicate their Reputations where I thought it due.

And

And some are not a little mistaken in their judgments of persons, if any Kingdom has at this time Two men of their Dignity, of more extraordinary Understandings : Which may (if well consider'd) be some inducement to their future preservation and esteem. As I have endeavour'd chiefly to clear their abuse, so I have pass'd divers considerable persons, under as malign inclinations of this Author's; conceiving, that what I have said for the Principals, may remove such smaller prejudices as are on the value of others on the same concern.

His most select and pecuniary Favourites, I have but barely touch'd, in respect his praise includes a concomitant reprehension , if well apprehended. Besides, I was unwilling to discourage any, that for the future may desire to be admir'd by him according to their liberality. A method, that perhaps may in time set up some Merchants of *Parnassus*, where the *Indies* of Fame seem lately discover'd, and may be purchas'd *per Centum*, according to modern example.

As to the Character of *Amiel*, I confess my Lines are something pointed, the one reason being, that it alludes much to a manner of expression of this Writer's, as may be seen by the marginal Notes; and a second will be soon allowed. The figure of *Amiel* has been so squeez'd into Paint, that his soul is seen in spite of the Varnish.

And none will deny, but it is as easie to send Truth backward, as it is to spur Falsities egregiously forward, and might have caus'd any Asse, as knowing as *Balaam's*, to have rebuk'd such a Poet as will needs

prophecy

prophecy againſt the ſenſe cf Heaven and Men. But
I have enough of this *Amiell*, as well as of his Muſe,
unleſs that by his means it occaſions a further account.
And for what is mine here, It will at worſt contraƈt
cenſure, in reſpeƈt it is a brief refleƈtion on a very
large Libel. And tho' I believe it did not coſt (tho'
that be not offer'd for an excuſe) the tenth part of
the time of the other. As to my Preface, I was willing that he ſhould find, that this ſmaller work has
ſome Noſe.---Tho' I am no more bound to have my
Face known by it, than he is willing to obſcure his by
a Nameleſs Preamble.

(1)

Poetical Reflections

ON A

POEM,

CALLED

Abſolon and Achitophel.

WHen late Protectorſhip was Canon-Proof,
    And *Cap-a-pe* had ſeiz'd on *Whitehall*-Roof.
    And next, on *Iſraelites* durſt look ſo big,
That *Tory-like*, it lov'd not much the *Whigg* :
A Poet there ſtarts up, of wondrous Fame ;
Whether *Scribe* or *Phariſee*, his Race doth name,
Or more t'intrigue the Metaphor of Man,
Got on a Muſe by *Father-Publican :*   A Com-
For 'tis not harder much, if we tax Nature,   mittee-
That Lines ſhould give a Poet ſuch a Feature ;   Man.
Than that his Verſe a *Hero* ſhould us ſhow,   Sir *Den-*
Produc'd by ſuch a Feat, as famous too.   *zill Hol-*
His Mingle ſuch, what Man preſumes to think,   *lis* ſeeks
But he can Figures daub with Pen and Ink,   *annus mi-*
A Grace our mighty *Nimrod* late beheld,   *rabilis.*

C   **When**

(2)

When he within the Royal Palace dwell'd,
And saw 'twas of import if Lines could bring
See his
Poem on
Gromwel. His Greatneſs from *Uſurper*, to be King:
Or varniſh ſo his Praiſe, that little odds
Should ſeem 'twixt him, and ſuch called Earthly Gods.
And tho no Wit can Royal Blood infuſe,
No more than melt a Mother to a Muſe:
Yet much a certain *P*oet undertook,
That Men and Manners deals in without-Book.
And might not more to Goſpel-Truth belong,
Than he (if Chriſtened) does by name of *John.*
This *P*oet, who that time much ſquanderd thought,
Of which ſome might bring Coyn, whilſt ſome none
As Men that hold their Brains of powerful ſenſe, (brought,
Will leaſt on Poet's Tales beſtow their pence,
Tho he ſuch Diſpenſations to endear,
Had notch'd his Sconce juſt level with his Ear.
An Emblem in theſe days of much import,
When Crop-ear'd Wits had ſuch a Modiſh Court.
Tho ſome from after-deeds much fear the Fate,
That ſuch a Muſe may for its Lugs create.
As Stars may without Pillories diſpence,
To ſlit ſome Ears for Forgeries of ſenſe,
Which Princes, Nobles, and the Fame of Men,
Sought to beſpatter by a worthleſs Pen.
But leaving this to Circumſtances fit,
With what thence ſpreads this Renegado-wit.
We'll tell you how his Court he now doth make,
And what choice Things and Perſons he doth take,
That Lines for Guinnys might more liquoriſh ſpeak.
To

To heigten which we'll to his Muse advance,
Which late difcover'd its *Judaick* Trance :
Where *Abfalon's* in *Englifh* Colours di'd,
That in a Duke, a Traitor might be fpi'd.
Or Heaven on him did Graces fo beftow,
As only could confer their Pageant Show ;
Giving his Glories no more faft Renown,
Than with more Honour to be taken down:
Like Victimes by fome Sacrificers dreft,
Muftfall adorn'd, which then they pity leaft.
But fear not *Monmouth*, if a Libel's quill,
Would dregs of Venom on thy Vertuefpill ;
Since no defert fo fmoothly is convey'd,
As next it's Fame, no canker'd Patch is laid ;
Thou didft no Honour feek, but what's thy due,
And fuch Heaven bids thee not relinqnifh too.
Whilft it's Impreffions fo oblig'd thy Task,
As leave from Earth thy Soul declin'd to ask.
If this thy Error were, what Influ'nce can
Excufe the Duty of more wilfull Man ;
With fuch whofe Figures fhew that fquinting Paint,
Whence peeps a Mungril *Babylonifh Saint*.
Thy Soul's Religion's Prop, and Native Grace,
Rome, (fears its onfets) looking on the place ;
What Altitude can more exalt thy Praife,
Tho beft Devotion fhould thy Trophies raife,
And 'tis perhaps from thy Diviner Blifs,
That fome may fear their Souls are feen amifs.
As what fo high does Emulation mount,
As Greatnefs when furpafs'd on Heaven's Account ;

And

(4)

And if th' Ambition would in this excel,
'Twas but to be more great in doing well;
And muft rebate the worft that Fates intend,
whilft Heaven and *England* is at once thy Friend.
This juft *Encomium*, tho too brief it be
To reprefent thy leaft Epitome;
And but unto thy larger Figure joyn'd,
As fmall proportions are from great defign'd;
Tho where a line one worth of thine can fpeak,
It does alone, a Poem's Greatnefs make;
Leaving this *Hero* to his fpotlefs Fame,
(As who befides this Wretch will it blafpheme)
Or in a Libels Allegorick way,
Men falfely figur'd, to the world convey,
Libels the enormous Forgery of fenfe,
Stamp'd on the brow of human Impudence;
The blackeft wound of Merit, and the Dart,
That fecret Envy points againft Defert.
The luft of Hatred pander'd to the Eye
T'allure the World's debauching by a Lie.
Th'rancrous Favourite's mafquerading Guilt,
Imbitt'ring venom where he'd have it fpilt.
The Courts depreffion in a fulfom Praife;
A Teft it's *Ignoramus* worft conveys,
A lump of Falfhood's Malice does difperfe,
Or Toad when crawling on the Feet of Verfe.
Fame's impious Hireling and mean Reward,
The Knave that in his Lines turns up his Card,
Who, tho no Rabby, thought in Hebrew wit,
He forc'd Allufions can clofly fit.

To

(5)

To *Jews* or *English*, much unknown before,
He made a *Talmud* on his Muses score;
Though hop'd few Criticks will its *Genius* carp,
So purely Metaphors King *David*'s Harp,
And by a soft Encomium, near at hand,
Shews *Bathsheba* Embrac'd throughout the Land.
But this Judaick Paraphrastick Sport
We'll leave unto the ridling Smile of Court.
Good Heav'n! What timeful Pains can Rhy-
    mers take,
When they'd for Crowds of Men much Pen-
    plot make?
Which long-Beak'd Tales and filch'd Allusions
    brings,
As much like Truth, as 'tis the Woodcock sings.
What else could move this Poet to purloin
So many *Jews*, to please the *English* Swine?
Or was it that his Brains might next dispense
To adapt himself a Royal Evidence?
Or that he'd find for *Dugdale*'s Wash some Spell,
In stead of once more dipp'd in *Winifred*'s Well;
And ope his Budget, like *Pandora*'s Box,
Whence Overt-acts more *Protestants* should Pox,
Which might the Joyner's Ghost provoke to rise,
And fright such Tales with other *Popish* Lies?
But *Starr*'s or *Ignoramus*'s may not give
Those Swearers longer swinge by Oaths to live.
A Providence much *English* Good protects,
And sends Testees to Trade for new Effects;
Which none of the Long-Robe, 'tis hop'd, can
    aid,
So well by Oaths the Devil's already paid;

D   And

And moſt ſuppoſe, if e're both Plots can die,
Or eat up one anothers Perjury,
'Twou'd *Pluto* ſtrangely poſe to find a Third,
Sould he in his a *Popiſh* Legion Lard.
A Policy ſome Poems much embrace,
As is diſcern'd in *Shaftsbury*'s Great Caſe;
Where Verſe ſo vile an Obloquy betray,
As for a Statiſt-*Jew* they'd him convey.
Tho hard it is to underſtand what Spell
Can conjure up in him *Achitophel,*
Or tax this Peer with an Abuſed Senſe
Of his ſo deep and apt Intelligence:
A Promptitude by which the Nation's ſhown
To be in Thought concurrent with his own.
Shaftsbury ! A Soul that Nature did impart
To raiſe her Wonder in a Brain and Heart;
Or that in him produc'd,the World might know,
She others did with drooping Thought beſtow.
As in Mans moſt perſpicuous Soul, we find
The neareſt Draught of her Internal Mind,
Tho it appears her higheſt Act of State,
When Human Conducts ſhe does moſt compleat,
And place them ſo,for Mankinds good,that they
Are fit to Guide, where others miſs their Way;
It being in Worldly Politiques leſs Great
To be a Law-maker, than Preſerve a State.
In Publick Dangers Laws are unſecure,
As ſtrongeſt Anchors can't all VVinds endure;
Though 'tis in Exigents the wiſeſt Eaſe
To know who beſt can ply whenStorms encreaſe;
VVhilſt other Proſpects, by miſtaking Fate,
Through wrong Preventions,more its Bad dilate.

                                        VVhence

(7)

Whence some their Counter-Politicks extend,
To ruine such can Evils best amend.
A Thwarting *Genius*, which our Nation more
Than all its head-strong Evils does deplore;
And shews what violent Movements such inform,
That where a Calm should be,they force a Storm;
As if their Safety chiefly they must prize
In being rid of Men esteem'd more Wise.
To this Great, Little Man, we'll T'other joyn,
Held Sufferers by one Tripartite Design.
As from a Cubick Power, or Three-fold Might,
Roots much expand, as Authors prove aright;
But of such Managements we'll little say,
Or shamm'd Intrigues, for Fame left to convey;
Which may by peeping through a Gown-mans
    Sleeve,
Tell such grave Tales, Men cannot well believe:
With what for Plots and Trials has been done,
As Whores depos'd, before away they run;
All which was well discern'd by numerous Sense,
Before the Doctors py'd Intelligence,
Who, with some Motley Lawyers,took much care
To gain the *Caput* of this Knowing Peer;
When after so much Noise, and nothing prov'd,
Heaven thank'd, to Freedom he's at last remov'd,
Leaving a Low-Bridge *Cerberus* to try
In what Clerks Pate his monstrous Fee does lie;
Or by the help of *Tory-Roger* tell
How Sacred Gain-Prerogativ'd should spell.
But these are Thoughts may fit some Pensive
    Skulls,
Or Men concern'd to bait their several Bulls;
                      Whilst

(8)

Whilft on this Peer we muft fome Lines beftow,
Tho more he merits than beft Verfe can fhow:
Great in his Name, but greater in his Parts,
Judgment fublim'd, with all its ftrong Deferts;
A Senfe above Occafions quick furprize,
That he no Study needs to make him Wife,
Or labour'd Thoughts, that trains of Sinews knit,
His Judgment always twin'd unto his Wit;
That from his clear Difcuffions Men may know
He does to wonder other Brains out-do.
VVhilft they for Notions fearch they can't com-
His *Genius* fitly ftands prepar'd to act.   (pact,
Admir'd of Man, that in thy Senfe alone
So ready doft exalt high Reafon's Throne;
That Men abate Refentments to expect
Thou mayft rife Greater, having paft Neglect.
A Sacred Method Kings receive from Heaven,
That ftill does Cherifh, when it has Forgiven;
Which from our Princes Soul fo largely flows,
That Mercy's Channel with his Greatnefs goes.
No Arbitrary Whifpers him can guide
To fwell his Rule beyond its genuine Tide:
Whilft other Kings their rugged Scepters fee
Eclips'd in his more foft Felicity;
Whofe Goodnefs can all Strefs of State remove,
So fitly own'd the Subjects Fear and Love.
My Verfe might here difcharge its hafty Flight,
As Pencils that attempt Immortal Heighth
Droop in the Colours fhould convey its Light,
Did not this Poet's Lines upon me call
For fome Reflexions on a Lower Fall;

Where

Where he by Rhyming, a *Judaick* Sham,
Obtrudes for *Israelites* some Seeds of *Cham*.
And this Infpexion needs no further go
Than where his Pen does moft Indulgent fhow:
And 'tis no wonder if his *Types* of Senfe
Should ftroke fuch *Figures* as give down their
    Pence;
A Crime for which fome Poets Lines fo ftretch,
As on themfelves they Metaphor *Jack Ketch*.
Tho fmall the Varnifh is to Humane Name,
Where Cogging Meafures rob the truth of Fame.
And more to do his skew'd *Encomiums* right,
Some Perfons fpeak by him their motly Sight:
Or much like *Hudibras*, on Wits pretence,
Some Lines for Rhyme, and fome to gingle Senfe.
Who elfe would *Adriel*, *Jotham*, *Hufhai*, fit,
With loathed *Amiell*, for a Court of VVit?
For, as Men Squares of Circles hardly find,
Some think thefe Meafures are as odly joyn'd.
VVhat elfe could *Adriell's* fharpnefs more abufe,
Than headlong dubb'd, to own himfelf a Mufe,
Unlefs to fpread Poetick Honours fo
As fhould a Mufe give each St. *George's* Show?
A Mode of Glory might *Parnaffus* fit,
Tho our Sage Prince knows few he'd Knight for
    VVit.
And thus this Freak is left upon the File,
Or as 'tis written in this Poet's Stile.
Next, as in Courfe, to *Jotham* we'll defcend,
Thoughtful it feems which Side he'll next be-
As thinking Brains can caper to and fro, (friend,
Before they jump into the Box they'd go.

68

And 'tis a moody Age, as many guess,
VVhen some with busie Fears still forward press;
As 'tis Ambitions oft-deluding Cheat
To tempt Mens aims, secureless of defeat.
Hushai the Compass of th' *Exchequer* guides,
Propense enough unto the North besides:
As what can steady Stations more allure,
Than such, a Princely Bed does first secure?
Whose Part none are so ignorant to ask,
And does no less employ his Ends and Task.
But quitting these, we must for Prospect pass
To gaping *Amiell*, as reflects our Glass.

* See his, p. 27. The *Him* indeed of his own * Western Dome,
So near his praiseful Poet Sense may come:

* See his, p. 28. For * *Amiell*, *Amiell*, who cannot endite
Of his *Thin* Value won't disdain to write?
The very *Him* with Gown and Mace did rule
The *Sanedrim*, when guided by a Fool.
The *Him* that did both Sense and Reason shift,
That he to gainful Place himself might lift.
The very *Him* that did adjust the Seed
Of such as did their Votes for Money breed.
The Mighty *Him* that frothy Notions vents,
In hope to turn them into Presidents.
The *Him* of *Hims*, although in Judgment small,
That fain would be the biggest at *Whitehall*.
The *He* that does for Justice Coin postpone,
As on Account may be hereafter shown.
If this plain *English* be, 'tis far from Trick,
Though some Lines gall, where others fawning
Which fits thy Poet, *Amiell*, for thy Smiles, (lick;
If once more paid to blaze thy hated Toils.

Of

(11)

Of Things and Perſons might be added more,
Without Intelligence from Forreign Shore,
Or what Deſigns Ambaſſadors contrive,
Or how the Faithleſs *French* their Compaſs guide:
But Lines the buſie World too much ſupply,
Beſides th'Effects of evil **Poetry**,
Which much to *Tory*-Writers ſome aſcribe,
Though hop'd no Furies of the *Whiggiſh* Tribe
Will on their Backs ſuch Lines or Shapes convey,
To burn with Pope, on Great *November's* Day.

F I N I S.

AZARIA

AND

HUSHAI,

A

POEM.

Quod cuique visum est sentiant.

LONDON,

Printed for *Charles Lee*,
An. Dom. 1682.

TO THE
READER.

I Shall not go about, either to excuse, or justifie the Publishing of this Poem; for that would be much more an harder Task than the Writing of it: But however, I shall say, in the words of the Author of the incomparable Absalom and Achitophel, That I am sure the Design is honest. If Wit and Fool be the Consequence of Whig and Tory, no doubt, but Knave and Ass may be Epithets plentifully bestowed upon me by the one party, whilst the other may grant me more favourable ones, than perhaps I do deserve. But as very few are Judges of Wit, so I think, much fewer of honesty; since Interest and Faction on either side, prejudices and blinds the Judgment; and the violence of Passion makes neither discernible in an Adversary. I know not whether my Poem has a Genius to force its way against prejudice: Opinion sways much in the World, and he that has once gained it writes securely. I speak not this any ways to lessen the merits of an Author, whose Wit has deservedly gained the Bays; but in this I have the advantage, since, as I desire not Glory or vain applause, I can securely wrap my self in my own Cloud, and remain unknown, whilst he is exposed through his great Lustre. I shall never envy what I desire not. nor am I altogether so doting, as to believe the Issues of my own Brain to exceed all others. and to be so very fond of them, (as most Authors, especially Poets, are) as to think them without fault, or be so blinded as not to see their blemishes, and that they are excelled by others; yet since Poems are like Children, it may be allowed me to be naturally inclined to have some good Opinion of my own, and not to believe this Poem altogether despicable or ridiculous. The Ancients say, that every thing hath two handles, I have laid hold of that opposite to the Author of Absalom: As to Truth, who has the better hold, let the World judge; and it is no new thing, for the same Persons, to be ill or well re-
presented

To the Reader.

presented, by several parties. I hope then, I may be excused as well as another, since I have told my Dreams with the same Liberty; for the fancies of Poets are no more than waking Dreams, and never imposed as dogmatical precepts, which are more agreeable to truth or falshood, or according to the Poets Language, which proceed from the Horny or Ivory Port, will be sentenced according to the Humour and Interest of several Parties who in spite of our Teeth will be our judges. Where I have been satyrical, 'tis without Malice or Revenge; and though I brag not of my Talent therein, I could have said much worse, of some Enemies to our Jewish Heroe. He that will lash others, ought not to be angry if the like be returned to himself: Lex talionis is a general and natural Law. I call not this an Answer to Absalom, I have nothing to do with him, he was a Rebel to his Father; my Azaria a good Son, influenced by a worthy and Loyal Counsellor, and Achitophel and Hushai were men of contrary Opinions, and different Principles: And if Poets (as it is often brought for their excuse, when they vary from known History) ought to represent Persons as they ought to be, I have not transcurred the Precepts of Poetry, and Absalom is not so good a Poem, because his Character is not so agreeable to the virtue of an Heroe, as this of Azaria is: But certainly when Poetry and Truth are joyned together, and that the Persons are truly what they are represented, and liv'd their Character, the glory is double, both to the Heroe and the Poet: And I could wish, that the same Hand, that drew the Rebellious Son, with so much Ingenuity and Skill, would out do mine, in shewing the virtues of an obedient Son and loyal Counsellor, since he may have as much Truth for a Foundation to build upon, the Artful Structure of the Heroes Glory, with his own Fame and Immortality.

AZARIA
AND
HUSHAI,

A POEM.

IN Impious Times, when Priest-craft was at height,
  And all the Deadly Sins esteemed light;
  When that Religion only was a Stale,
  And some bow'd down to God, and some to *Baal*;
When Perjury was scarce esteem'd a Sin,
And Vice, like flowing Tides, came rowling in;
When Luxury, Debauch, and Concubine,
The sad Effects of Women and of Wine,
Rag'd in *Judea* and *Jerusalem*,
Good *Amazia* of great *David's* Stem,
God-like and great in Peace did rule that Land,
And all the *Jews* stoop'd to his just Command.
Long now in *Sion* had he Peace enjoy'd,
After that Civil Broils the Land destroy'd:
Plenty and Peace attended on his Reign,
And *Solomon's* Golden days return'd again;
When the Old *Canaanites*, who there did lurk,
Began to find both God and King new Work:
For *Amazia*, tho' he God did love,
Had not cast out *Baal's* Priests, and cut down every Grove.
Too oft Religion's made pretence for Sin,
About it in all Ages Strife has been;

B   But

But Int'reft, which at bottom doth remain,
Which ftill converts all Godlinefs to Gain,
What e'er Pretence is made, is the true Caufe,
That moves the Prieft, and like the Load-ftone draws.
The *Canaanites* of Old that Land poffefs'd,
And long therein Idolatry profefs'd ;
Till Sins of Priefts, and of the Common Rout,
Caus'd God and his good Kings to caft them out.
Their Idols were pull'd down, their Groves deftroy'd,
Strict Laws againft them, and their Worfhip made.
The Heathen Priefts were banifh'd from the Land
Of *Baal*, no Temple fuffer'd was to ftand ;
And all Succeeding Kings made it their Care,
They fhould no more rear up their Altars there.
If fome mild Kings did wink at their Abode,
They to the *Jews* ftill prov'd a Pricking-goad :
Growing more bold, they penal Laws defy'd,
And like tormenting Thorns, ftuck in their Side.
The bufy Priefts had loft their gainful Trade,
Revenge and Malice do then Hearts invade ;
And fince by Force they can't themfelves reftore,
Nor gain the Sway they in *Judea* bore,
With Hell they Joyn their fecret Plots to bring
Deftruction to *Judea* and its King.

The *Chemerarims*, the learnedft Priefts, of all
The numerous Swarms which did belong to *Baal*,
Bred up in fubtil Arts, to *Jews* well known,
And fear'd for Bloody Morals of their own ;
Who in the Caufe of *Baal* no one would fpare,
But for his fake on all Mankind make War,
Counting it lawful Sacred Kings to fmite,
Who favor'd not their God, or was no *Baalite*,
Thefe were the Idol's known, and great Support,
Who in Difguife creep into every Court,
Where they foon Faction raife, and by their Arts.
Infinuate into the Princes Hearts :
Wriggle themfelves into Intreagues of State,
Sweet Peace deftroy, and Bloody Wars create.

Unwearied

Unwearied ftill, they deep Defigns purfue:
What can't a *Chemarim*, and *Belzeebub* do?
For cunning Plot, Trepan, for Oaths and Sham,
The Devil muft give place to *Chemarim.*
Thefe fubtil Priefts, in Habit black and grave;
Each man a Saint in fhew, in Heart a Knave,
Did in *Judea* fwarm, grew great withall,
And like th' *Egyptian Frogs* to Court they crawl:
Where, like them too, they never are at reft;
But Bed and Board of Kings, with Filth infeft.
To every Shape they could themfelves transform,
Angels could feem, but ftill their Aim was Harm.
They all the Sects among the *Jews* could ape,
And went about difguifs'd in every Shape.
One imitates the *Zealous Pharifee*,
The *Effens* this, the dammee *Sadduce* he;
And fuch their ready, and their fubtil Wit,
For every Trade, and every Science fit:
They Credit got, and ftole into the Heart,
And from their God, did many Souls pervert,
Who feeming *Jews*, or what they were before,
In Secret did the Idol *Baal* adore;
Whofe falfe Religion was but loofe, and few
Could bear the Righteous Strictnefs of the true.

Thus thefe Difciples of the hellifh Brood,
Difguis'd, among the *Jews*, themfelves intrude,
And with the purer Wheat, their Tares they fow,
Saw their bad Crop near to an Harveft grow,
And hop'd that they again fhould rule the State:
For e'er the days of good *Jehofaphat*,
Through all the Land *Baal's* Worfhip was allow'd,
And King and People to grofs Idols bow'd.
The Priefts, like Bloody Tyrants did command;
They and their Gods, did wholly rule the Land;
And every one who would not bow to *Baal*,
Fled thence, or elfe by Fire, or Sword did fall:
But that good King a Reformation made,
Their Idols, and their Groves he quite deftroy'd;
In every place their Altars overthrew,

B 2   And

And *Chemarims* he banished or flew.
Since when (except in *Athaliah*'s Reign,
Who for a fpace, fet Idols up again,
Tormenting thofe to Death who would not turn,
And did the *Jewifh Rabbins* flay or burn)
Thefe crafty Priefts, by Plots did never ceafe,
To fpoil the Beauty of *Judea's* Peace.
Whilft *Joafh* reign'd, by fly and fubtil Arts,
They firft eftrang'd from him his Peoples Hearts.
Saw Faction's Sparks, and unfeen blew the Fire,
Till Rebells 'gainft that good King did confpire :
Then Curfed *Zabed* of proud *Ammon's* Line,
And *Moabitifh Jehozabad* joyn,
And to their Side fome *Pharifees* they drew,
(*Joafh* did to their Sect no Favor fhew)
And th' *Effens*, who then daily numerous grew,
Rebell, and their good King, like Murtherers, flew.
Then *Amazia* over *Jordan* fled,
Till God had ftruck the Tyrant *Zabed* dead;
When all his Subjects, who his Fate did moan,
With joyful Hearts, reftor'd him to his Throne;
Who then his Father's Murtherers deftroy'd,
And a long, happy, peaceful Reign enjoy'd.
Belov'd of all, for merciful was He,
Like God, in the Superlative Degree.
The *Jewifh* Sects he did not feek to quell,
Yet Laws he made they might no more rebell :
Wifely about them made of Laws a Fence,
Yet kind, would not opprefs their Confcience.
The *Pharifee*, a very numerous Sect,
Above the reft were in their Worfhip ftrict :
In their own *Synagogues* he let them pray,
And worfhip God after their ftricter way.
In Peace all liv'd, and former ftrife forgot,
The *Chemarims* and Hell had hatch'd a Plot :
A Plot form'd in the deep Abyfs below,
Law and Religion both to overthrow.
The King was by their Bloody Swords to fall,
That all *Judea* might fubmit to *Baal*.

Great

Great were their Hopes, and deep was their Design.
The Train already laid to spring their Mine ;
Not dreaming Heav'n could their Plots betray,
They only waited an auspicious day.
Nor fail'd their Plot for want of Common Sence,
As some endeavor'd to persuade the Prince :
For with much Art, great Industry and Care,
They all things for their black Design prepare.
Not hatch'd by Common Brains, or men of Earth,
Nor was't the Issue of a suddain Birth ;
But long designing, and well laid it seems,
By Baal's Arch-priests, and subtil Chemarins.
The Canaanites dispersed through the Land,
O'er whom Baal's Priests had absolute Command,
Were bound with Oaths, the Priests Religious Charms,
To Secresie, and furnished with Arms.
Heads they had got, as well as Hands to fight,
Some zealous Princes of the Canaanites,
Who ready were to guide the Common Rout,
So soon as their Conspiracy broke out.
Ægypt of Warlike Jews was still afraid,
Lest as of Old, they should that Land invade,
To further this Design had promis'd Aid.
Thus on a firm Foundation they had wrought
Their great Design, well built to Humane thought :
Tho' nothing that weak Mortals e'er design'd,
But Folly seems to the Eternal Mind,
Who blasting man's vain Projects, lets him know,
He sits above, sees and rules all below.
This wicked Plot, the Nations Bain and Curse,
So bad no man can represent it worse :
Want only Amazia to destroy,
But that they might the Rites of Baal enjoy :
For the good Amazia being gone,
They had design'd a Baalite for the Throne.
Of all their Hopes and Plots, here lay the Store :
For what Encouragement could they have more,
When they beheld the King's own Brother fall,
From his Religion, and to worship Baal ?

The Prieſt well knew what Pow'r, and what Controul
He had uſurp'd o're ev'ry *Baalite*'s Soul,
That ſuch a Prince muſt their God's Cauſe purſue,
And do whatever they would have him do;
Elſe from his Throne he ſhould be curs'd and damn'd:
For *Baal*'s High-Prieſt, a Right t' all Crowns had claim'd.
An Article 'tis of a *Baalite*'s Faith,
That o're Crown'd Heads a Sovereignty he hath.

Thus on a ſure Foundation, as they thought,
They had their Structure to Perfection wrought
When God, who ſhews regard to Sacred Kings,
The Plot and Plotters to Confuſion brings,
And in a moment down their *Babel* flings.
A *Levite*, who had *Baalite* turn'd, and bin
One of the Order of the *Chemarim*,
Who in the Plot had deeply been concern'd,
And all their horrid Practices had learn'd;
Smote in his Conſcience with a true Remorſe,
From King and Land diverts the threat'ning Curſe.
Libni, I think they call'd the *Levite*'s Name,
Which in *Judea* ſtill will be of Fame ;
Since following Heaven's Impulſe and high Command,
He prov'd a Glorious Saviour of the Land.
By him the deep Conſpiracy's o'rethrown,
The Treaſon, and the Traytors all made known :
For which from *Baalites* he had Curſes ſtore;
But by the *Jews* loaded with Bleſſings more.
The Helliſh Plotters were then ſeiz'd upon,
And into Goals and Iron Fetters thrown ;
From whence to Lawful Tryals they were born,
Condemn'd for Traytors, and hang'd up with Scorn:
Yet *Chemarims* with matchleſs Impudence,
With dying Breath avow'd their Innocence:
So careful of their Order they ſtill were,
Leſt Treaſon in them Scandal ſhould appear,
That Treaſon they with Perjury purſue,
Having their Arch-prieſt's Licence ſo to do.
They fear'd not to go perjur'd to the Grave,
Believing their Arch-prieſt their Souls could ſave:

For

For all God's Power they do on him beftow,
And call him their Almighty God below.
To whom they fay three powerful Keys are given,
Of Hell, of Purgatory, and of Heav'n.
No wonder then if *Baalites* this believe,
They fhould, with their falfe Oaths try to deceive,
And gull the People with their Dying Breath,
Denying all their Treafon at their Death.
This made Impreffion on fome eafie Minds,
Whom or good Nature, or falfe Pity blinds;
Mov'd their Compaffion, and ftirr'd up their Grief,
And of their dying Oaths caus'd a Belief.
This did effect what the curs'd Traytors fought,
The Plots Belief into Difcredit brought,
Of it at firft, fome Doubts they only rais'd,
And with their Impudence the World amaz'd:
Tho' *Azyad*'s Murder did the *Jews* convince,
Who was a man moft Loyal to his Prince,
And by the Bloody *Chemarims* did fall,
Becaufe he feiz'd the Trayt'rous Priefts of *Baal*:
Tho' *Gedaliah*'s Letters made all plain,
Who was their Scribe, and of a ready Brain:
A *Levite's* Son, but turn'd a *Baalite*,
Who for the King's own Brother then did write,
And Correfpondence kept i'th' *Egyptian* Court,
To whom the Traytors for Advice refort;
Who like a zealous, trayt'rous *Baalite* dy'd,
And at the Fatal Tree the Plot deny'd.
Tho' *Amazia* did at firft believe,
And to the Hellifh Plot did Credit give;
Tho' the Great Council of the *Sanhedrim*,
Among the *Jews* always of great Efteem,
Declar'd to all the World this Plot to be,
An Hellifh, and a curs'd Confpiracy,
To kill the King, Religion to o'rethrow,
And caufe the *Jews* their Righteous Laws foregoe;
To make the People to dumb Idols fall,
And in the place of God, to fet up *Baal*:
Tho' all the People faw it, and believ'd;
Tho' Courts of Juftice, hard to be deceiv'd,

Had

Had added to the reſt their Evidence,
Yet with a ſtrange unheard of Impudence,
The *Baalites* all ſo ſtoutly had deny'd
Their Helliſh Plot, with Vows and Oaths beſide,
And with ſuch Diligence themſelves apply'd.
They at the laſt, their ſought for point had got,
And artfully in doubt had brought their Plot.
A thouſand cunning Shams and Tricks they us'd,
Whereby the ſimple Vulgar were abus'd;
And ſome o'th' *Edomitiſh* Evidence,
Who *Mammon* worſhip'd, were brought off with pence.
Libni, for whom, before their Harps they ſtrung,
Who was the Subjeƈt of each *Hebrew*'s Song,
Was villify'd by every Raſcall's Tongue.
In Secret, and inglorious did remain,
And the Plot thought the Projeƈt of his Brain.

The *Baalites* thus encourag'd by Succeſs,
Increaſe their Hopes, and their black Projeƈts bleſs:
Like the bold *Titans*, Plot on Plot they lay,
And Heav'n it ſelf with impious Arms eſſay.
A new Invention wrought in Hell below,
The *Jews*, and their Religion to o'erthrow;
They bring to light, with this their Hopes they raiſe,
And for dire Plots, think they deſerve the Bays.
This Engine ſtronger than th' old *Roman* Ram
For Battery, by a new name call'd Sham,
With well learn'd, and ſucceſsful Arts they uſe
To overthrow the *Syn'gogues* of the *Jews*,
Their Worſhip and Religion to confound.
And lay their Glorious Temple on the Ground.
With this new Engine, they a Breach had made,
By which they hop'd the Loyal *Jews* t' invade.
With Troops of Treaſons, and Rebellious Plots,
Led on by Villains, perjur'd Rogues and Sots;
And with ſuch Arms, in Hells black Work-houſe form'd,
The peaceful *Jews* they violently ſtorm'd;
Who 'gainſt the *Ba'lites* Plots had no defence,
But God, their Laws, and their own Innocence.

Among

Among the Princes of the *Jewish* Race,
For Wisdom, *Hushai* had the Chiefest Place,
Prudent in Speech, and in his Actions close;
Admir'd by all, and feared by his Foes;
Well skill'd, and knowing in the *Jewish* Laws,
Able to plead, and to defend a Cause,
Of piercing Judgment, and of pregnant Wit,
Did once Chief Judge of all *Judea* sit;
Was then esteem'd the Honor of the Gown,
And with his Vertues sought to serve the Crown,
Till Foes procur'd him *Amazia's* Frown.
Then he descended from the hight of Place,
Without a Blemish, and without Disgrace;
Yet inly griev'd; for he could well divine
The Issue of the *Baalites* curs'd Design,
To see Religion, and God's Righteous Cause,
The Ancient Government, the Nation's Laws,
Unpropping, and all ready strait to fall,
And the whole Race of *Jews* made Slaves to *Baal* :
With Zeal inspired, boldly up he 'rose,
To wrestle with the King's, and Nation's Foes;
And tho' he was with Wealth and Honor blest,
He scorn'd to give his Age its needful Rest:
He learn'd, that man was not born for himself,
To get great Titles, Names, or sordid Pelf,
To wear a lazy Life, himself to please,
With Idleness, and with luxurious Ease :
When he beheld his Country in distress,
And none the Danger able to redress,
He did resolve, tho' not affecting Fame,
Or to obtain a Patriot's Glorious Name,
His Rest, his Life, his Fortune to expose,
Rather than see his Countrey's dangerous Foes
Run on uncheck'd, till they had brought the Land,
To their, and to a *Baalite* King's Command.
He could not therefore so himself forget,
To see the Barques of Government o'erset ;
But with his Skill he help'd the Boat to trim,
And boldly did oppose *Eliakim.*
C

Eliakim was Brother to the King,
From the fame Loins, and Royal Seed did fpring ;
Of Courage bold, and of a daring mind,
To whom the King, ev'n to Excefs was kind ;
And tho' he had a Son, for him the Crown defign'd.
Sweet *Azaria*, like the beauteous Morn,
Whence all Sweets flow, did once that Court adorn,
A budding Rofe, whofe Beauty's newly blown,
Or like a Cedar on Mount *Lebanon :*
He in his Father's Grace, and Favor grew,
And towards him the People's Eyes he drew.
He was by moft belov'd, admir'd by all,
For's Zeal to God, and's Hatred unto *Baal :*
But ah! this mov'd the curfed *Baalite's* Hate,
Difturb'd his Peace , and Troubles did create.
What can't Defign and Hellifh Malice do?
With Lyes they clofe this Noble Prince purfue.
They think his Father too indulgent grown,
Whofe Love had many Bleffings on him thrown,
But what exceeded all the reft befide,
He chofe the fweet *Jerufha* for his Bride:
A Blefling he efteemed far above
The Crown, and all things but his Father's Love:
For that he ftill above his Life did prize,
Dear as his Fame, and dearer than his Eyes.
Below his Feet, for that he all things trod,
Adoreing nothing more except his God.
Young as he was, he had acquired Fame,
His Breaft infired with a Warlike Flame,
In Foreign Wars, his Courage he had fhown,
Had Lawrels won, and brought home fair Renown :
Happy, moft happy, till with wondrous Art,
His Foes had wrought him from his Father's Heart;
And fo much Power on *Amazia* won,
He by Degrees, grew jealous of his Son.
And who for this can *Amazia* blame,
If that the King the Father overcame?
For Crowns by Kings efteemed are more near,
Than Children, or than Sons, belov'd more dear.

His

His Foes, *Baal's* Friends, had laid their artful Snairs,
Hight'ned his Father's Jealousies and Fears,
And made each innocent Action of the Prince,
To give his Jealous Father an Offence.
If with wise *Hushai* they the Prince did see,
They call'd their Meeting a Conspiracy,
And cry, that he was going to rebell:
Him *Absalom* they name, *Hushai Achitophel.*
With Slander thus the Prince they did pursue,
Aiming at's Life, and the wise *Hushai's* too.
When they much pleas'd, and triumphing saw,
The King his Royal Favors to withdraw,
Which like a Spring on him before did flow,
And from him, all on others to bestow:
Defenceless left, naked, almost forlorn,
Subject to every trifling Rhimers Scorn,
And beyond *Jordan* by their malice drove,
No Succor left him but the People's Love ;
(For he was still their Darling and Delight,
Because they saw he was no *Baalite*,)
Their Hopes now almost at their Height did seem,
To place the Crown upon *Eliakim.*

The *Jews*, God's People and peculiar Care,
For their true Worship still most zealous were;
That Jewel seem'd most pretious in their Eyes,
And it above all Humane things they prize.
No Torments could make them their Faith deny,
They willingly for their Religion die:
Their Liberties were also dear to them,
Sprung from a free, and not a slavish Stem,
Th' *Egyptian* Bondage for their Souls unfit,
They never in *Judea* would permit;
Their own known Laws, they willingly obey,
Hate Tyranny and Arbitrary Sway:
Nor did they many Priviledges want,
Kept from the Time they first the Land did plant;
For which to Death they lawfully would strive,
If injur'd by their King's Prerogative:

For fome of them have try'd to break the Bound,
And did like *Ethnick* Kings, their People's Freedom wound,
So *Rehoboam* caus'd them to rebell,
And loft at once ten Tribes of *Ifrael*.
No people were more ready to obey
Their Kings, who rul'd them by a gentle Sway,
Who never fought their Confciences to curb,
Their Freedom or Religion to difturb.
To fuch they always open-hearted were,
For them, they neither Coin, nor Blood would fpare.
Such Kings might their Prerogatives improve,
And rule the *Jews*, ev'n as they pleas'd with Love;
But ftiff indeed they were, and moody grew, }
When Tyrants did with cruel Stripes purfue
Them fore opprefs'd, and fometimes murmur'd too. }
Kings they had try'd of ev'ry fort and fize.
Beft govern'd by the Warlike and the wife.
Tho' Kings they lov'd, and for them Reverence had,
They never would adore them as a God.
God's Worfhip, and their Laws they did prefer,
They knew, them men might by bad Councils Err.
Tho' Loyal, yet opprefs'd, they did not fear
To make their heavy Grievances appear.
This was indeed the Humor of the *Jew*,
The People by Complaints their Griefs would fhew;
And never would, in truth, contented feem,
Untill redrefs'd by their wife *Sanhedrim*.
Thus now the *Jews*, tho' free from ill Defign,
In their Religious Caufe together joyn:
They caft their Eyes on *Amazia*'s Son,
Who, without Arts the People's Love had won:
Full of tormenting Jealoufies and Fears,
Eliakim a dangerous man appears:
The fober part of the whole *Sanhedrim*,
Defire to keep *Judea*'s Crown from him:
For they forefaw if he fhould wear the Crown,
Baal's Worfhip he'd fet up, and God's caft down:
That all the Nations muft be Slaves to *Baal*,
Suffer in Flames, fly, or 'fore Idolls fall.

Great

Great were their Fears, but yet they did abhor
The very Thought of a dishonest War :
For they had seen the Kingdom's many Scarrs,
Th' unseemly Marks of former Civil Wars.
They *Amazia* lov'd and wish'd him well,
Resolve to suffer rather than rebell;
Yet openly declare free from all Stain,
How much they hate a *Baalite* should Reign;
And for this Cause, and for this Cause alone,
Eliakim they'd put by from the Throne.

Eliakim at Court had many Friends,
By whom in Secret he could work his Ends;
So that no Accusation could remove
Him, deeply rooted in his Brother's Love.
But since the *Jews* to him shew'd open Hate,
Left that his presence should embroil the State;
And that the *Jews* might have no cause to sin,
He's sent to rule the Tribe of *Benjamin*.
Thus two great Factions in *Judea* rose,
So hotly each the other did oppose,
  Twas fear'd they'd fall at last from Words to Blows.
Each side most zealous for the King appears,
Each full of Jealousies and disturbing Fears,
Each pleads for *Amazia* and the Laws,
God and Religion both do make their Cause :
Both Loyalty profess, both opposite,
Both would persuade that each was in the right,
Tho' both contrary shew as day and night.
Sweet *Azaria* with these Troubles mov'd,
On that side hated, and by this belov'd ;
Fearing th' inveterate Malice of his Foes,
Which he sought to avoid, not to oppose,
And left they should their sought Occasion find,
To tax him of an ill ambitious mind,
By seeing all the *Jews* to him so kind ;
Left he should grow i'th' King's Opinion worse,
He seeks for Council how to steer his Course,
That he might to the Court give no Offence,
But live wrapt up in his own fair Innocence,

The

88 [14]

The wife and thoughtful *Hufbai* he doth find,
And thus to him he breaks his troubled Mind,
Great Councellor, and Favorite of Heav'n,
To whom the Bleffing of true Wifdom's giv'n,
Which by no Mortal can poffeffed be,
Whofe Thoughts are not inform'd by Loyalty.
I know Reproaches upon you are thrown;
But judge your Innocency by my own.
I am accufed Sir, as well as you,
And the fame Foe doth both our Lives purfue.
He fears your Wifdom, may his Hndrance prove,
And me, becaufe I have the People's Love:
His Creatures therefore throw on you and me,
The Scandal of a curs'd Confpiracy,
Againft our King and Father to rebell :
Me *Abfalom*, and you *Achitophel*
They name; bad Councellor, and worfer Son,
Who Traytors, durft into Rebellion run.
My Father governs with fo equal Sway,
That all both love him, and his Laws obey:
He feems Heav'n's Care, who fet him in the Throne,
Preferved by his wondrous Power alone.
Oh may on him no Blemifh fall or ftain,
But all live happy in his peaceful Reign :
May he be happy ftill as he is good,
Like God in Mercy, not inclin'd to Blood.
This is the Prayer that I daily make ;
For Piety fhall never me forfake,
Tho' I his Royal Favor ne'er partake.
And tho' my Foes have with their fubtil Art
Banifh'd me from my Royal Father's Heart,
Which is the Source of all my Grief and Woe,
My juft Obedience I will ne'er forgoe.
Nor has Difgrace, nor my hot Paffions wrought,
Within my Breaft one bad diffloyal Thought.
I ne'er believ'd my Father would betray
H's People, or fought Arbitrary Sway :
Or tho' his People did his Wrath provoke,
He meant to curb them with an Iron Yoak.

Yet

Yet do I think, nay more than think, the Caufe
(But here his paffion made fome little paufe,
Till fighing, at the laft he thus went on)
Why my Great Father does difown his Son ;
They fay I am but of a fpurious Brood,
My Mother being of Ignoble Blood:
For *Jocoliah* was but mean by Birth,
Tho' with the King fhe mix'd her bafer Earth.
I was begotten in my Father's Flight,
E'er to the Crown he had obtain'd his Right:
And fince I from his Favor did decline,
He has declar'd her but his Concubine.
This has the Hopes rais'd of *Eliakim*,
And *Amaziah*'s Crown defign'd for him ;
My Hopes are loft, and I do think it fit,
I fhould to God, Right, and the King fubmit ;
But yet, wife *Hufhai* know, I ftill do find,
My Birth has not fo much debas'd my mind,
To make me ftoop to low or mean defires ;
I feel my Father's Royal Blood infpires
My deprefs'd Soul, wipes off th' ignoble Stain,
Renders me apt, or not unfit to reign.
Of *David*'s Royal Blood, my felf I own,
And with it never can difgrace the Throne.
Tho' my bold Spirits, mounting thus, do fly.
Towards the Noble hight of Sovereignty,
And that I feel my Father's Blood to rowl
Through every Vein and animate my Soul ;
Yet fo much Loyalty is fown within
My Breaft, I would not Empire gain with Sin:
For when my ambitious Thoughts begin to roam,
Their Forces, I with that foon overcome.
Tho' to God's Laws, and to the King's I yield,
To my known Foes I would not leave the Field.
I'd not be trampl'd on by fordid Feet,
Nor take Affronts from ev'ry one I meet:
I'd give no Caufe they fhould my Courage doubt,
Nor to Rebellion pufh the vulgar Rout,
I to my Father would give no Offence,
Nor while he lives, lay to the Crown Pretence ;

But

But since Life's sweet, by Wisdom I'd keep mine,
From *Baalites* Hate, and *Eliakim*'s Design :
This my wise Friend, is my chief Business now,
To take some Sage and good Advice from you.

  Hushai in Silence heard the Prince, and weigh'd
Each word he spake, then to him thus reply'd ;
Great Prince, th' Almighty has to you been kind,
Stamp'd Graces on your Body and your mind,
As if he for your Head a Crown design'd.
We shall not search into Fates Secret Womb,
God alone knows the things that are to come ;
But should you never sit on *David*'s Throne,
'Tis better to deserve than wear a Crown.
Of Royal Blood, and of great Birth you are,
Born under some benign auspicious Star,
Lov'd by the best, and prais'd by every Tongue,
The glorious Subject of each worthy Song :
The young man's Wish, Joy of each Warlike Wight,
The People's Darling, and the World's Delight.
A Crowd of Vertues fill your Princely Breast,
And what appears more glorious than the rest,
You are of Truth and Loyalty possest.
That I would cherish in you, that would raise
To an admired height, that I would chiefly praise.
Let Fools and subtil Politicians scorn
Fair Vertue, which doth best a Prince adorn :
Whilst you her bright and shining Robes put on,
You will appear more great than *Solomon*.
Let not Great Prince, the Fumes of Vulgar Praise,
Your bolder Spirits to Ambition raise.
We cannot see into the Mist of Fate,
Till time brings forth, you must expecting wait ;
But Fortune, rather Providence, not Chance,
The constant, stout, and wise doth still advance.
Let your quick Eye be to her Motions ty'd ;
But still let Noble Vertue be your Guide :
For when that God and Vertue points the way,
There can be then no danger to obey.
But here in Wisdom's School we ought to learn,
How we 'twixt Good and Evil may discern,

For

For, noble Prince, you muſt true difference make,
Leſt for the one the other you miſtake.
You muſt not think you may your ſelf advance,
By laying hold on every proffer'd chance.
Tho Fortune ſeems to ſmile, and egg you on,
Let Vertue be your Rule and Guide alone.
Thus *David* for his Guide his Vertue took ;
Nor was by Fortune's proffer'd Kindneſs ſhook.
His Vertue and his Loyalty did ſave
King *Saul*, when Fortune brought him to his Cave.
And if that I may to you Counſel give,
You ſhould without a Crown for ever live,
Rather than get it by the Peoples Luſt,
Or purchaſe it by ways that are unjuſt.
David your Anceſtor, from whom you ſpring,
Would never by Rebellion be made King ;
But long in *Gath* a Warring Exile ſtay'd,
Till for him God a lawful way had made.
In *Hebron*, full of Glory and Renown,
He gain'd, at laſt, and not uſurpt the Crown.
By full Conſent he did the ſame obtain,
And Heav'n's anointing Oyl was not in vain.
I once did ſeem to *Amazia* dear,
Who me above m'ambitious hopes did rear ;
I ſerv'd him then according to my ſkill,
And bow'd my Mind unto my Soveraign's Will.
Too neer the Soveraign Image then I ſtood,
To think that every Line and Stroke was good.
Some Daubers I endeavour'd to remove,
And to amend their artleſs Errours ſtrove.
My Skill in ſecret theſe with ſlander wound ;
With every Line I drew ſtill faults were found ;
Till wearied, I at laſt my Work gave o're. ⎫
And *Amazia* (I ſhall ſay no more)   ⎬
Did me to my lov'd Privacy reſtore.   ⎭
For this they think I muſt my Vertue change,
For Envy, Malice, and for ſweet Revenge.
Me by themſelves they judge, who would do ſo,
And cauſe the King ſuſpect me for his Foe.

D

But by th'advice I give, you beſt will find
Th'Integrity and Plainneſs of my Mind ;
And that I harbour not that vile intent
Their Poets and their Malice do invent.
Far be't from me, to be like Curſed *Cham* ;
A good Son ſtrives to hide his Father's ſhame.
A King, the Father of his Country is ;
His ſhame is every Aĉt he doth amiſs.
Good and juſt Kings God's Image bear ; but when
Their Frailties let us ſee they are but Men,
We cannot every Aĉtion ſo applaud,
As if it came from an unerring God.
Kings have their Paſſions, and deceiv'd may be,
When b'others Ears and Eyes they hear and ſee :
For Sycophants, of Courts the Bane and Curſe,
Make all things better than they are, or worſe.
To Evil prone, to Miſchief ever bent,
Th'all Objeĉts with falſe colours repreſent ; }
The Guilty clear, condemn the Innocent.
Thus, noble Prince, they you and me accuſe
With all the Venome Malice can infuſe.
Baal's Prieſts, Hell, and our Foes, new Arts have got,
The filthy Reliques of their former Plot ;
Whereby they would our Lives in danger bring,
And make us curſed Traytors to the King.
What mayn't theſe cunning men hope to atchieve,
When by their Arts few men their Plot believe ?
When b'horrid ways, not known to *Jews* before,
Their Plot's transform'd, and laid now at our door ?
But fear not, Sir, we have a ſure Defence,
The Peoples Love, God, Law, and Innocence.
Keep faſt your Vertue, and you ſhall be bleſt,
And let alone to God and Time the reſt.
    The Noble Youth, with Vertues Robes arrai'd,
Conſider'd well what the wiſe *Huſbai* ſaid.
Deſire of Power, though of Celeſtial Birth,
Below, is ever intermixt with Earth :
And all who do to hight of Place aſpire,
Have earthly Smoak mixt with their mounting Fire.

Praiſe

Praife may debauch, and ftrong Ambition blind,
Where heav'nly Vertue does not guard the Mind.
But *Azaria* fo well underftood,
He left the Evil, and embrac'd the Good :
Tho in his breaft afpiring thoughts he found,
Yet Loyalty ftill kept them within bound.
And tho he might have Empire in his Eye,
When to it by his bloud allay'd fo nigh,
Yet in his Soul fuch Vertue did remain,
He by Rebellion would not Empire gain.
Through every Vein his Loyal Bloud did run,
Yet Royal too, as *Amazia's* Son.
About his noble Heart he felt it fpring ;
Which let him know his Father was a King.
If that to *Azaria* were a Blot,
His Father made it when he him begot :
But Heav'n fuch Virtue moulded with his Soul,
That his afpiring Luft it did controul.
Thus to wife *Hufbai* he repli'd : I finde
Your Counfel is agreeing with my Minde.
And tho my Foes me an ill man do make,
My Loyalty I never will forfake :
Yet, prudent *Hufbai*, do not Nature blame,   ⎫
If I cannot, unmov'd, appear fo tame   ⎬
As not to fhew Refentment at my Shame.   ⎭
Oh, would to Heav'n I ne'er had been begot !
Or never had been born a Royal Blot!
My Father's Bloud runs thorow every Vein ;   ⎫
He form'd thofe Spirits which defire to reign, ⎬
Mount t'wards a Throne, and fordid Earth difdain. ⎭
In Glory, Fame, Crowns, Empire, they delight,
And to all thefe they would affert my Right.
And my great Thoughts do whifper there is none
Can be more neer a Father, than his Son.
This prompts me to oppofe *Eliakim*,
And never yield my Father's Crown to him.
But then one groveling thought ftrait pulls me down,
And throws me at a diftance from the Crown.
Oh, would to God------And here he ftopt and figh'd,
Whilft *Hufbai* thus to the griev'd Prince repli'd.

                                        Indeed

Indeed, great Prince, it seemeth wondrous strange
To all the World, to see your Father's change;
To find the happy Love he us'd to show'r,
Like fruitful Rain, on you, to fall no more:
To see a Son, the Father's dear Delight,
His pleasing Joy, now banish'd from his sight.
Nature must in the Father deeply groan,
When from his Heart is rent so dear a Son.
Nor can I think, tho he from you should part,
A Brother e'er can lie so near his Heart.
To work this Change, your Foes much Art do use, ⎫
Their venom'd Tongues your Fathers Ears abuse, ⎬
And you of an aspiring mind accuse. ⎭
Justice in *Amazia* bears such sway,
That even Nature must to it give way;
H'ad rather Nature force, and part with you,
Than seem to rob another of his due.
He holds it just, and as a thing divine,
To keep unbroken still the Royal Line.
Such an Example we can hardly find,
A King to's Brother so exceeding kind;
When by it he doth such great hazard run,
Losing at once his People and his Son.
Grieve not, great Prince, at your unhappy Fate; ⎫
Let not your Birth your Vertue to abate; ⎬
It was not you that could your self create. ⎭
I should great folly shew, should I repine
At what I could not help, and was no fault of mine.
Tho by your Mothers side your Birth was mean,
And tho your Mother no declared Queen,
If Heaven and your Father please, you may
By lawful Right, *Judea's* Scepter sway,
After that he is number'd with the Dead,
And his great Soul to *Abraham's* Bosom fled.
Possession of a Crown clears every Stain;
No blot of Birth to you can then remain.
What Pow'r on Earth, by Right, dares question you?
Or what your Father and *Sanhedrim* do?
Nor is your Birth to Heaven any let;
God *Jepthtah* once did o're *Judea* set.

He

He was a Conquerour of a mighty Name,
And's Mother no ways did eclipfe his Fame,
Nor bar'd him from the Title of a King,
Nor thofe who after from his Loins did fpring.
Nature may yet make your great Father kind;
And who can tell but he may change his mind,
When your Succeffion fhall be underftood
To be the Peoples Choice, and for the Nations Good?
But let us leave what is to come, to Fate;
Yours Father's pleafure and God's will await.
Long may it be ere the King's life doth end;
On it our Peace and Happinefs depend.
Like Wheat full ripe, with many years bow'd down,
Let him leave this for an immortal Crown.
And who can tell Heav'n's will? it may be too,
Eliakim may die before the King or you.
Think of no Titles while your Father lives;
Take not what an unjuft Occafion gives.
For to take Arms you can have no pretence,
Tho it fhould be e'en in your own defence.
It better were without the Crown to die,
Than quit your Vertue and bleft Loyaltie.
You with the numerous Peoples Love are bleft,
Not of the Vulgars onely, but the Beft.
I would not have you their kind Love repel,
Nor give encouragement for to rebel:
For their Affection which they wildly fhew,
Is rendred, by your Foes, a Crime in you.
Here you your Courfe muft even fteer and ftrait,
That you may not your Father's fears create;
Keep the *Jews* Love, and not increafe his Hate.
Leave for a while the Citie and the Court,
Go and divert your felf with Country-fport;
Perhaps your Foes may then abate their fpight,
And you may be forgot, when out of fight.
By your Retirement, you will let them fee
You'd take away all caufe of Jealoufie.
That you, like *Abfalom*, will never prove,
To court the head-ftrong Peoples factious Love.

Nor

Nor will I ever prove *Achitophel*,
To give you wicked Counſel to rebel.
Continue ſtill your Loyalty, be juſt ;
And for the Crown, God and your Vertue truſt.
Endeavour not to take what may be giv'n ;
Deſerve it firſt, and then receive't from Heav'n.

He ſaid, And this Advice above the reſt,
Suited with *Azaria's* Vertue beſt.
He was not ſtain'd with Cruelty or Pride;
A thouſand Graces he poſſeſt beſide.
To Vertue he was naturally inclin'd,
And Goodneſs clothed his heroick Mind.
His Kingly Vertues made him fit to reign,
Yet ſcorn'd by evil Arts the Crown to gain.
And tho he Empire to deſire did ſeem,
His Loyalty was ſtill more dear to him :
Therefore he did not court the Peoples Love,
Nor us'd their Pow'r his Rival to remove.
From's Father he ſought not their Hearts to ſteal,
Nor head a Faction mov'd by blinding Zeal ;
But like a vertuous and a pious Son,
Sought all occaſions of Offence to ſhun.
In private like a common man ſat down,
His Peace his Rule, his Loyalty his Crown.

Thus humble, vertuous, loyal, void of Pride,
Moſt of the *Jews* he gained to his ſide.
Not factious Sects, the Rabble, or the rude
Erring, unthinking, vulgar Multitude :
But the chief Tribes and Princes of the Land,
Who durſt for *Moſes's* ancient Statutes ſtand.
The pious, juſt, religious, and the good,
Men of great Riches, and of greater Bloud,
Did, as one man, themſelves together joyn
To ſtop the *Baalites*, and Hell's curſt deſign.
Not wicked, or ſeduc'd by impious Arts,
But Loyal all, and Patriots in their Hearts.
For they beheld the *Baalites* foul intent,
Religion to o'rethrow and Governmenr.

Theſe

These at the Monarch's Power did not grutch,
Since bound by Laws, he could not have too much.
What Laws prescribe, they thought he well might have,
How could he else his Realm in danger save?
But *Baal's* or *Egypt's* Yoke they would refuse,
Not fitting for the Necks of free-born *Jews*.
They all resolve the King not to oppose,
Yet to defend the Nation from its Foes.
And were it not for those great Worthy men,
The *Jews* distress'd and wretched soon had been.
Among the Rout perhaps there some might blend,
Whose int'rest made them Publick Good pretend;
Weary of Peace, new Troubles would create,
And for their private Gain, embroyl the State.
And some perhaps there were, who thought a King
To be of Charge, and but an useless thing.
Some idle Fops, who publickly debate
To shew their Parts, the deep Intrigues of State;
These and some others, for a Commonwealth,
Among the Herd, unseen, might hide by stealth:
But it would strange to common Justice seem,
For some few bad, the sound Flock to condemn.
Like Goats among the Sheep, well known these bleat,
And are like Darnel 'mong the purest Wheat.
These not as Friends, but Enemies to the Throne,
Good Patriots and good Subjects did disown.
And *Azaria*, tho tehy us'd his name,
Disdain'd their Friendship with a loyal shame.

But he beheld appearing on his side,
Princes, whose Faith and Loyalty were try'd;
Such as no base or sordid ends could move,
Who did his Father and their Country love.
In the first rank of these did *Nashon* stand,
None nobler or more loyal in the Land.
Under the King he once did *Edom* sway,
And taught that Land the *Jews* good Laws t'obey.
True to his Word, and of unspotted Fame;
Great both in Parts, in Vertue, and in Name.

His

His Faith ne'r touch'd, his Loyalty well known,
A Friend both to his Country and the Throne.
Bafe ends his great and noble Soul did fcorn,
Of loyal, high, and noble Parents born.
His Father with renown and great Applaufe,
For *Joaſh* di'd, and fuffer'd for his Caufe.
Of great *Aminadab* who would not fing,
Whofe glory fhin'd next to the martyr'd King?
From him his Son true Loyalty underftood,
Impreft on's Soul, feal'd with his Father's Bloud.
The grave, religious, wife, rich *Helon* too,
Much honoured by every zealous *Jew*,
Appear'd a Patriot, to his Country true.
In the *Jews* Laws, and ftrict Religion bred,
And *Baal's* curft Rites did much abhor and dread.
His Son *Eliab*, in the *Sanhedrim*,
With courage had oppos'd *Eliakim:*
A man whofe many Vertues, and his Parts,
Had won upon the fober Peoples Hearts.
From every Faction, and from Envy free;
Lov'd well the King, but hated Flatterie;
Kept *Mofes's* Laws, yet was no *Pharifee.*
He went not to their *Synagogues* to pray,
But to the Holy Temple every day.
With piercing Judgment faw the Lands Difeafe,
And labour'd onely for the Kingdoms Peace:
Loyal and honeft was efteem'd by all,
Excepting thofe who ftrove to fet up *Baal.*
For an ill Action he ne'r ftood reprov'd;
But's King, his Country, and Religion lov'd.
No Taint ere fell upon *Eliab's* name,
Nor Hell it felf found caufe to fpot his Fame.
Pagiel with honour loaded, and with years,
Among this Loyal Princely Train appears.
None *Pagiel* tax'd, for no one ever knew
That he to *Amazia* was untrue.
A Fame unfpotted he might truly boaft;
Yet he had Foes, and his gain'd Favours loft.
Zuar, a fober and a vertuous Prince,
Who never gave leaft caufe of an offence.

Eli-

Elisbama, at once both sage and young,
From noble and from loyal Fathers sprung, ⎫
Shone bright among this sober Princely throng. ⎬
Enan, a Prince of very worthie Fame; ⎭
Great in deserved Title, Bloud, and Name.
Elizur too, who number'd with the best
In Vertue, scorn'd to lag behind the rest.
Abidon and *Gamaliel* had some sway;
Both loyal, and both zealous in their way.
And now once more I will invoke my Muse,
To sing brave *Ashur's* praise who can refuse?
Sprung from an ancient and a noble Race,
With Courage stampt upon his manly face;
Young, active, loyal; had through Dangers run,
And with his Sword abroad had Honours won:
Well-spoken, bold, free, generous, and kind,
And of a noble and discerning mind.
Great ones he scorn'd to court, nor fools would please,
But thought it better for to trust the Seas.
He thought himself far safer in a Storm,
And should receive from raging Seas less harm,
Than from those dangerous men, who could create
A Storm at Land, with Envie and with Hate.
And now got free from all their Trains and Wiles, ⎫
He at their hateful Plots and Malice smiles, ⎬
Plowing the Ocean for new Honour toils. ⎭
These were the chief; a good and faithful Band ⎫
Of Princes, who against those men durst stand ⎬
Whose Counsel sought to ruine all the Land. ⎭
With grief they saw the cursed *Baalites* bent
To batter down the *Jewish* Government;
To pull their Rights and true Religion down,
By setting up a *Baalite* on the Throne.
These wisely did with the *Sanhedrim* joyn;
Which Council by the *Jews* was thought divine.
The next Successour would remove, 'tis true,
Onely because he was a *Baalite* Jew.
Ills they foresaw, and the great danger found, ⎫
Which to the King (as by their Dutie bound) ⎬
They shew'd, and open laid the bleeding Wound. ⎭

But such who had possest his Royal Ear,
Had made the King his Loyal Subjects fear ;
Did their good Prince with causeless terrour fright,
As if these meant to rob him of his Right.
Said, They with other Rebels did combine,
And had against his Crown some ill designe :
That the wise *Hushai* laid a wicked Train,
And *Azaria* sought in's stead to reign :
That the old Plot to ruine Church and State,
Was born from *Hushai's* and the *Levite's* Pate :
That *Pharisees* were bold and numerous grown,
And sought to place their Elders in his Throne.
No wonder then if *Amazia* thought
These Loyal Worthies did not as they ought ;
That they did Duty and Obedience want,
And no Concessions from the Throne would grant.

They who in *Amazia's* favour grew,
Themselves obnoxious to the People knew.
Some were accused by the *Sanhedrim*,
Most Friends and Allies to *Eliakim* :
For his Succession eagerly they strove,
And him, the rising Sun, adore and love.
When *Doeg*, who with *Egypt* did combine,
And to enslave *Judea* did designe,
Accus'd of Treason by the *Sanhedrim*,
Kept in the Tower of *Jerusalem* ;
The Object prov'd of fickle Fortunes sport,
And lost the Honours he possest at Court.
Elam in favour grew, out stript by none,
And seem'd a Prop to *Amazia's* Throne.
He had in foreign parts been sent to School,
And did in *Doeg's* place the Kings thin Treasure rule.
He to *Eliakim* was neer alli'd ;
What greater parts could he possess beside ?
For the wise *Jews* believ'd the King did run
Some hazard, if he prov'd his Father's Son.
But now, alas ! th' Exchequer was grown poor,
The Coffers empty, which did once run o're.

The

The bounteous King had been so very kind,
That little Treasure he had left behind.
Elam had gotten with the empty Purse,
For his dead Father's sake the Peoples Curse :
For they believ'd that no great good could spring
From one false to his Country and his King.
Jotham the fickle Shuttle-cock of Wit,
Was bandied several ways to be made fit :
Unconstant, he always for Honour tri'd,
At last laid hold upon the rising side.
If Wit he had, 'twas thought, by not a few,
He a better thing did want, and Wisdom too.
Then *Amiel* would scarce give place to him,
Who once the chief was of the *Sanhedrim.*
He then appeared for the Crowns defence ;
But spoke his own, and not the Nations sense.
And tho he praised was by *Shimei's* Muse,
The *Jews* of many Crimes did him accuse.
Harim, a man like a bow'd Ninepence bent,
Had tried all the ways of Government :
Was once a Rebel, and knew how to cant ;
Then turn'd a very Devil of a Saint :
Peevish, morose, and some say, prov'd a fool,
When o're the *Edomites* he went to rule.
When to his bent the King he could not bring,
He fairly then went over to the King.
Old *Amalack,* a man of cunning head,
Once in the cursed School of Rebels bred ;
From thence his Maximes and his Knowledge drew,
Of old known Arts how to enslave the *Jew.*
For pardon'd Treason, thus sought to atone,
Had wrong'd the Father, would misguide the Son.
Once in Religion a strict *Pharisee,*
To *Baal's* then turn'd, or else of none was he.
He long before seem'd to approve their Rites,
Marrying his Issue to the *Baalites.*
A constant hunter after sordid Pelf ;
Was never just to any but himself :
A very *Proteus* in all shapes had been,
And constant onely, and grown old in sin.

To ſpeak the beſt of *Amalack* we can,
A cunning Devil in the ſhape of Man.
Muppim, a man of an huge working Pate,
Not how to heal, but to embroil the State ;
Knew how to take the wrong, and leave the right ;
Was once himſelf a Rebel *Benjamite*.
To that ſtiff Tribe he did a while give Law,
And with his iron Yokes kept them in aw.
The Tyrant *Zabed* leſs did them provoke,
And laid upon their necks a gentler Yoke.
Amongſt that Tribe he left an hated Name,
And to *Jeruſalem* from thence he came ;
Where he tyrannick Arts ſought to intrude,
To learn which, *Amazia* was too good,
And better the *Jews* temper underſtood.
Refus'd, the Serpent did with Woman joyn,
And Counſels gave th'*Egyptian* Concubine.
Adam, firſt Monarch, fell between theſe two ;
What can't the Serpent and a Woman do ?
Theſe with ſome more of the like ſize and ſort,
In *Sion* made up *Amazia*'s Court :
Whilſt his beſt friends became theſe Rulers ſcorn,
Saw how they drove, and did in ſilence mourn.
Sion did then no Sacrifice afford ;
Gibbar had taught the frugal King to board.
Void were its Cellars, Kitchins never hot,
And all the Feaſts of *Solomon* forgot.
Others there were, whoſe Names I ſhan't repeat ;
Eliakim had friends both ſmall and great :
And many, who then for his Favour ſtrove,
With their hot heads, like furious *Jehu*, drove.
Some Wits, ſome Witleſs, Warriors, Rich and Poor,
Some who rich Clothes and empty Titles wore ;
Some who knew how to rail, ſome to accuſe,
And ſome who haunted Taverns and the Stews.
Some roaring Bullies, who ran th'row the Town
Crying, God damn 'um, they'd ſupport the Crown :
Whoſe wicked Oaths, and whoſe blaſphemous Rant,
Had quite put down the holy zealous Cant.

Some

Some were for War, and some on Mifchief bent;
And fome who could, for gain, new Plots invent.
Some Priefts and Levites too among the reft,
Such as knew how to blow the Trumpet beft :
Who with loud noife and cackling, cri'd like Geefe,
For Rites, for Temple, and for dearer Fleece.
'Twixt God and *Baal*, thefe Priefts divided were ;
Which did prevail, thefe greatly did not care ;
But headlong drove, without or wit or fear.
The *Pharafees* they curfe, as Sons of *Cham*,
And all diffenting *Jews* to Hell they damn.
Shimei the Poet Laureate of that Age,
The falling Glory of the *Jewifh* Stage,
Who fcourg'd the Prieft, and ridicul'd the Plot,
Like common men muft not be quite forgot.
Sweet was the Mufe that did his wit infpire,
Had he not let his hackney Mufe to hire :
But varioufly his knowing Mufe could fing,
Could *Doeg* praife, and could blafpheme the King :
The bad make good, good bad, and bad make worfe,
Blefs in Heroicks, and in Satyrs curfe.
Shimei to *Zabed*'s praife could tune his Mufe,
And Princely *Azaria* could abufe.
Zimri we know he had no caufe to praife,
Becaufe he dub'd him with the name of *Bays*.
Revenge on him did bitter Venome fhed,
Becaufe he tore the Lawrel from his head ;
Becaufe he durft with his proud Wit engage,
And brought his Follies on the publick Stage.
Tell me, *Apollo*, for I can't divine,
Why Wives he curs'd, and prais'd the Concubine ;
Unlefs it were that he had led his life
With a teeming Matron ere fhe was a Wife :
Or that it beft with his dear Mufe did fute,
Who was for hire a very Proftitute.
The rifing Sun this Poets God did feem,
Which made him tune's old Harp to praife *Eliakim*.
Bibbai, whofe name won't in Oblivion rot,
For his great pains to hide the *Baalites* Plot,

Muft

Muſt be remembred here : A Scribe was he,
Who daily damn'd in Proſe the *Phariſee*.
With the Sectarian *Jews* he kept great ſtir ;
Did almoſt all, but his dear ſelf, abhor.
What his Religion was, no one could tell ;
And it was thought he knew himſelf not well :
Yet Conſcience did pretend, and did abuſe,
Under the notion of Sectarian *Jews*,
All that he thought, or all that did but ſeem
Foes to *Baal's* Rites, *Eliakim*, and him.
He was a man of a pernicious Wit
For railing, biting, and for miſchief fit :
He never ſlept, yet ever in a Dream ;
Religion, Law, and State, was all his Theam.
On theſe he wrote in *Earneſt* and in *Jeaſt*,
Till he grew mad, and turn'd into a Beaſt,
Zattue his Zanie was, Buffoon, and Fool,
Who turn'd Religion into Ridicule :
Jeer'd at the Plot, did *Sanhedrims* abuſe,
Mock'd Magiſtrates, damn'd all Sects of the *Jews*.
Of little Manners, and of leſſer Brains ;
Yet to embroil the State, took wondrous pains.
In jeaſting ſtill his little Talent lay ;
At *Huſhai* ſcoſt in's witleſs grinning way.

Theſe with the reſt, of every ſize and ſort,
Strove to be thought Friends to the King and Court,
With lyes and railing, would the Crown ſupport.
Then in a Pageant ſhew a Plot was made,
And Law it ſelf made War in Maſquerade.
But fools they were, not warn'd by former ill,
By their own ſelves were circumvented ſtill.
They thought by Bloud to give the Kingdom eaſe :
Phyſick'd the *Jews* when they had no Diſeaſe.
Contingent miſchiefs theſe did not foreſee,
Againſt their Conſcience fought, and God's Decree.
What ſhall we think, when ſuch, pretending good,
Would build the Nations Peace on Innocent Blood?
Theſe would expoſe the People to the Sword
Of each unbounded Arbitrary Lord.

But

But their good Laws, by which they Right enjoy,
The King nor could, nor ever would deftroy.
And tho he Judge be of what's fit and juft,
He own'd from Heaven, and from Man a Truft.
Tho Laws to Kingly Power be a Band,
They are not Slaves to thofe whom they command.
The Power that God at firft to *Adam* gave,
Was different far from what all Kings now have :
He had no Law but Will ; but all Kings now
Are bound by Laws, as all Examples fhow.
By Laws Kings firft were made, and with intent
Men to defend, by Heav'n's and Man's confent.
God to the Crown the Regal Power did bring,
And by Confent at firft, Men chofe their King.
If Kings ufurp'd a Power, by force did fway,
The People by no Law were bound t'obey.
This does not in the People place a Right
To diffolve Soveraign fway by force or might.
To Kings, by long fucceffion, there is giv'n
A native Right unto the Throne, by Heav'n :
Who may not be run down by common Cry,
For Vice, Oppreffion, and for Tyranny.
But if that Kings the tyes of Laws do break,
The People, without fault, have leave to fpeak ;
To fhew their Grievances, and feek redrefs
By lawful means, when Kings and Lords opprefs.
Tho they can't give and take, whene'r they pleafe,
And Kings allow'd to be God's Images.
The Government you Tyranny muft call,
Where Subjects have no Right, and Kings have all.
But if reciprocal a Right there be,
Derived down unto Pofteritie,
That fide's in fault, who th'other doth invade,
By which foe'r at firft the breach is made :
For Innovation is a dangerous thing,
Whether it comes from People or from King.
To change Foundations which long Ages ftood,
Which have prov'd firm, unfhaken, found, and good,
To pull all down, and caft the Frame anew,
Is work for Rebels, and for Tyrants too.

Now

Now what relief could *Amazia* bring,
Fatal indeed to be too good a King?
Friends he had many, but them did not know,
Or else made to believe they were not so :
For all that did ill Ministers oppose,
Were represented to him as his Foes.
Yet there were many thousands in those days,
Who *Amazia* did both love and praise ;
Who for him daily pray'd, and wish'd his good,
And for him would have spent both Coin and Bloud.
Yet these, tho the more numerous, and the best,
Were call'd but murmuring Traytors by the rest :
By such who strain'd till they had crackt the string
Of Government ; lov'd Pow'r, and not the King
These daily hightned *Amazia*'s fears,
And thus they whisper'd in his Royal Ears :

Sir, it is time you now take up the Sword,
And let your Subjects know you are their Lord.
Goodness by Rebels won't be understood,
And you are much too wonderful and good.
The *Jews*, a moody, murmuring, stubborn Race,
Grow worse by Favours, and rebel with Grace.
Pamper'd they are, grown rich and fat with ease,
Whom no good Monarch long could ever please.
Freedom and Liberty pretend to want ;
That's still the cry, when they're on Mischief bent.
Freedom is their Disease ; and had they less,
They would not be so ready to transgress.
Give them but Liberty, let them alone,
They shall not onely you, but God dethrone.
Remember, Sir, how your good Father fell ;
It was his goodness made them first rebel.
And now the very self-same tract they tread,
To reach your Crown, and then take off your head.
A senseless Plot they stumbl'd on, or made,
To make you of th'old *Canaanites* afraid.
Still when they mean the Nation to enthral,
With heavie Clamour they cry out on *Baal*.

But

But these hot Zealots who *Baal's* Idols curse,
Bow to their own more ugly far and worse.
Baal would but rob some Jewels from your Crown,
But these would Monarchy itself pull down :
Both Church and State they'l not reform by Halves,
Pull down the Temple, and set up their Calves.
You, and your Priests, they would turn out to Graze,
Nor would they let you smell a Sacrifize,
Those pious Offerings which Priests lasie made,
To Rebels, should, instead of God be paid.
How to the Prey these factious *Jews* do run!
From you by art they have debauch,d your Son ;
That little subtle Instrument of Hell,
Worse than to *David* was *Achitophel*,
The young Man tutors, sends him through the Land,
That he the peoples minds may understand ;
That he, with winning Charms, might court the *Jew*,
And draw your fickle Subjects hearts from you.
Alas ! already they of you Complain.
And are grown sick of your too peaceful Reign,
Their Lusts grown high, they are debauch'd with Grace,
And like unfrozen Snakes fly in your Face.
These men who now pretend to give you Law,
Stood of the Tyrant *Zabed's* power in awe ;
He made them crouch who scorn'd a Prince's sway,
And forc'd them, like dull slaves, his power obey.
Of *Israel*, and of *Juda's* Tribe you spring,
A Lion is the Ensign of a King,
Rouse up your self, in mildness sleep no more,
And make them tremble at your princely roar :
Appear like *Jove* with Thunder in your hand,
And let the Slaves your power understand ;
Strike but the sinning Princes Down to Hell,
The rest will worship you, and ne'r rebel.

　　Thus these rash Men with their bad Counsels strove,
To turn to hate good *Amazia's* Love.
A Prince to Mercy naturally inclin'd,
Not apt to fear, nor of a Jealous Mind,
Thought no Man e'r against his Life design'd,

R

But thefe with Art did dangers reprefent,
And Plots they fram'd the People never meant.
Each Mole hill they a Mountain did create,
And fought to fright him with his Fathers Fate.
Hufhai at laft was to a Prifon fent,
As a falfe Traitor to the Government.
Loud murmurs then poffeft the troubled *Jews,*
Who were furprifed at the fatal News;
His Wifdom they believed their chief fupport,
Againft the evil Inftruments at Court;
Nor, by his Actions, did they ever find,
He bore a Trait'rous, or a factious Mind:
And now they thought themfelves expos'd to all
The Arts, and Plots of the hid friends to *Baal.*
Troubled, and difcontented, at the laft,
Their Eyes upon the noble Prince they caft.
Who fearing left their difcontent and rage,
Should them, to fome rebellious Crime ingage,
Both for his Fathers, and his Countries fake,
The murmuring People fought more calm to make.
With a fweet Air, and with a graceful look,
He did command their filence, e'er he fpoke,
Then thus he faid, and though his words were few,
They fell like Manna, or the Hony Dew;
    My Country-men, Let not your difcontent
Draw you to actions you will foon repent,
What e'er your fears and jealoufies may be,
Let them not break the bonds of Loyalty.
I dare, and you may too, my Father truft,
For he's fo merciful, fo good, fo juft,
That he of no mans Life will make a Prey,
Or take it in an Arbitrary way,
To Heav'n, and to the King fubmit your caufe,
Who never will infringe your ancient Laws;
But if he fhould an evil Action do,
To run to Arms, 'tis no pretence for you.
The King is Judge of what is juft and fit,
And if he judge amifs you muft fubmit,
Tho griev'd you muft your conftant duty pay,
And your Redrefs feek in a lawful way.

Hushai tho he of Treason be accus'd,
Such loyal precepts in my soul infus'd,
That I the hazard of my life will run,
Rather than prove my self a Rebel Son.
Our Foes, have fought to' infect my Father's mind,
To think, you to Rebellion are inclin'd :
To stir you to Rebellion is their aim,
And they are mad, to see you justly tame.
Upon your Heads, they fain would lay their sin,
'Tis War they seek, but would have you begin :
Pretence they want, who for the King do seem,
To bring in, and set up *Eliakim.*
I am afraid the *Baalites* cursed Plot,
By many laught at, and by most forgot,
Is carried on still, in their hidden Mine,
I fear, but dare not, the event, divine.
May Heav'n defend my Father's Life, and late,
Full ripe with Age, in peace, may he' yield to Fate.
I know, my Friends, for Him's your chiefest Care,
For him, as much as for your selves, you fear,
Upon his Life our happiness depends,
With it the peace of all *Judea* ends,
Be vigilant, your foes Designs prevent,
Let not loud murmures shew your discontent :
Your Loyal Duty to your Soveraign pay,
Your Griefs present him in a Lawful way :
Be not too anxious for our common Friend,
God, and his Innocence will him defend :
Sit down in quiet, murmure not, but pray,
Submit to Heaven, your King, and Laws obey.
Youth, Beauty, and the Grace wherewith he spoke,
The Eyes, Ears, Hearts, of all the people took,
Their murmures then to joyful shouts were turn'd,
And they rejoyc'd, who lately murmuring mourn'd :
With Loyalty he did their Breasts inflame,
And they with shouts blest *Azaria*'s name.
The joyful Cry th'row all the City flew,
God save the King, and *Azaria* too.
To him the Princes, his best Friends resort,
Resolv'd as Suppliants, to repair to Court ;

In humble wise, to shew the King their Grief,
And on their bended Knees to seek Relief.
They 'approach'd the Throne, to it their homage paid,
Then to the King, the Loyal *Nashon* said.
Great Sir, whom all good Subjects truly Love,
Tho all things that you do they can't approve,
We, whom the Throne has with high Honours blest,
Present you here the prayers of the rest:
Our bended Knees, as low as Earth we bow,
And humbly prostrate supplicate you now :
The blessing of your Love to us restore,
And raise us to your Favour, Sir, once more.
Where is the Joy, the Peace, and Quiet flown,
All had, when first you did ascend the Throne ;
Now murmuring discontents assault our Ears,
And loud Complaints of jealousies, and fears:
Bad instruments help to blow up this Fire,
And with ill minds, their own worse Arts admire,
Whilst, by their means, you think your Friends your Foes,
For your best friends, your Enemies suppose ;
Suspect your Loyal Subjects, and believe
The *Sanhedrim* would you of Rights bereive.
Your people, who do love your gentle Sway,
And willingly their God, and you obey,
Who for Religion ever zealous were,
For that, for you, and for themselves do fear.
Clear as the Sun, by sad effects they find,
A *Baalite* to succeed you is design'd :
Sir, they would not dispute with you, his right,
But they can n're indure a *Baalite:*
Tho whilst you live, they are secure and blest,
Yet are they with a thousand fears opprest,
Think your Life still in danger of the Plot,
Which now is laugh'd at, and almost forgot.
They see the *Baalites* Hellish Plot run down,
And on the *Pharisees* a false one thrown ;
Your zealous faithful *Jews* all Rebels made,
Their ruine hatch'd, you, and themselves betray'd.
Oh ! Sir, before things to extreams do run,
Remember, at the least, you have a Son,

Let

Let the *Sanhedrim* with your wifdom joyn,
To keep unbroken ftill the Royal line ;
And to fecure our fears, that after you,
None fhall fucceed but a believing *Jew.*
Sir, this is all your Loyal Subjeḋs Crave,
On you, as on a God, they cry to fave.
Kings are like Gods on Earth, when they redrefs,
Their peoples Griefs, and fave them in diſtreſs.
With loads of careful thoughts, the King oppreſt,
And long revolving in his Royal Breaſt,
Th' event of Things-----at laſt he filence broke,
And, with an awful Majeſty, he fpoke.
I 've long in Peace *Judeas* Scepter fwaid,
None can Complain, I Juſtice have delay'd :
My Clemency, and Mercy has been fhown,
Blood, and Revenge did ne'r pollute my Throne ;
I and my People happy, kindly ftrove,
Which fhould exceed, my Mercy or their Love :
Who, till of late, more ready were to give
Supplies to me, than I was to receive.
Oh ! happy days, and oh ! unhappy change ;
That makes my *Sanhedrims,* and my people ftrange,
And now, when I am in the Throne grown old,
With grief I fee my Subjeḋs Love prove cold.
They fear not my known Mercy to offend,
And with my awful Juſtice dare contend ;
But yet their Crimes my mercy fhan't affwage,
I'm ready to forgive th' offending Age,
And though they fhould my Kingly power flight,
I'le ftill keep for them my forgiving right.
I feel a tendernefs within me fpring,
I am my Peoples Father, and their King,
And tho I think, they may have done me wrong.
I can't remember their offences long.
Nature is mov'd, and fues for a Reprieve,
They are my Children, and I muft forgive.
My many jealous fears I fhan't repeat,
My Heart with a ftrong pulfe of Love doth beat;
Nature I feel has made a fudden ftart,
And a frefh fource fprings from the Father's heart.

A

A stubborn Bow, drawn by the force of men,
The force remov'd, flies swifty back agen.
'Tis hard a Fathers nature to o'ercome,
How easily does she her force assume!
Sh'has o'er my Soul an easie Conquest won,
And I remember now I have a Son,
Whose Youth had long been my paternal Care,
Rais'd to the height his noble frame could bear,
And Heav'n has seem'd to give his Soul a turn,
As if ordain'd by Fate for Empire born.
By our known Laws I have the Scepter sway'd,
By them I govern'd, them my Rule I made.
To them I sought to frame my soveraign Will,
By them my Subjects I will govern still:
They, not the People, shall proclaim my Heir, ⎫
Yet I will hearken to my Subjects Prayer, ⎬
And of a *Baalite* will remove their fear. ⎭
From hence I'le banish every Priest of *Baal*,
And the wise *Sanhedrim* together call:
That Body with the Kingly Head shall join,
Their Counsel and their Wisdom mix with mine,
All former strife betwixt us be forgot,
And in Oblivion buried every Plot.
We'l try to live in Love and Peace again,
As when I first began my happy Reign.
Before our Trait'rous Foes with secret toil
Did fair *Judea*'s blessed Peace embroil.
May all my latter days excel my first,
And he who then disturbs our Peace be curst.

He said: Th' Almighty heard, and from on high
Spoke his Consent, in Thunder through the Skie:
The Augurie was noted by the Croud,
Who joyful shouts return'd almost as loud:
Then *Amazia* was once more restor'd,
He lov'd his People, they obey'd their Lord.

FINIS.